GERALD O'COLLINS SJ AC

LETTERS TO MAEV

A THEOLOGIAN & HIS SISTER

Published by Connor Court Publishing, 2023.

CONNOR COURT PUBLISHING PTY LTD
PO Box 7257
Redland Bay QLD 4165
sales@connorcourt.com

www.connorcourtpublishing.com.au

Cover design by Ian James, cover image: Maev at her desk in Canberra.

ISBN: 9781922815446

Printed in Australia

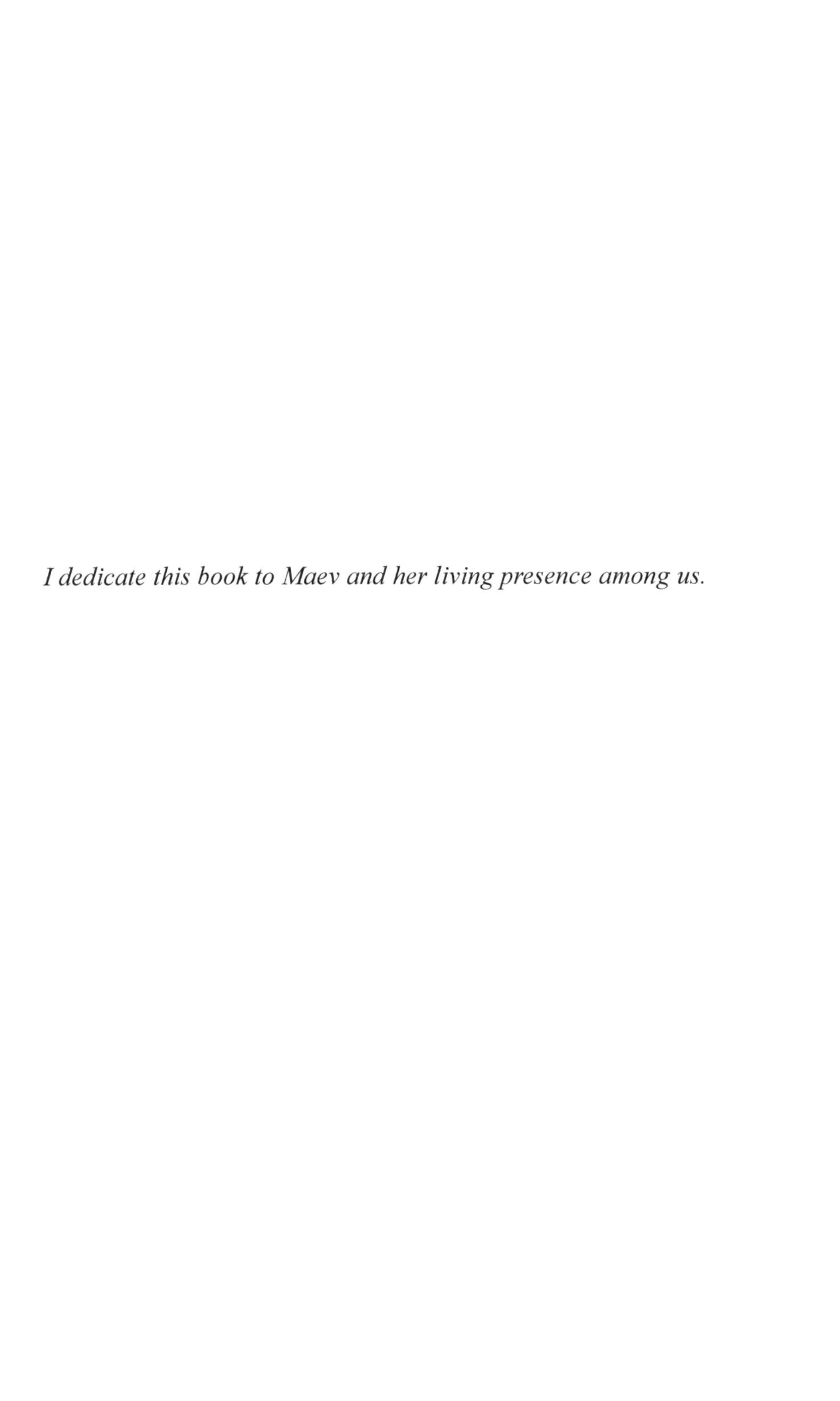

I dedicate this book to Maev and her living presence among us.

Maev at her family home, 'Rock Lodge' (Frankston South, Victoria), with Dympna and Gerald on left, baby Glynn centre, and Moira and Jim right: early 1935.

Preface

'If you don't marry, have an interesting life.' That was Mother's advice to her third daughter and my sister, Ellen Maev O'Collins (1929–2021). As a social worker in Melbourne (1952–67), Maev certainly enjoyed an interesting life. She became a principal officer for adoptions, and helped hundreds of children and parents become happy families. With other social workers she developed adoption practices that became laws which better protected the rights of adopting parents and their children.

Maev's life flowered in her doctoral studies at Columbia University (New York, 1967–72) and then in her academic teaching and leadership at the University of Papua New Guinea (Port Moresby, 1972–89), and, finally, over more than two decades in Canberra at the Australian National University and Australian Catholic University.

Maev's life was also an *inspiring* life—for her nephews and nieces, who often travelled with her or stayed with her, and, in particular, for me. Two years younger, I drew on her wisdom, energy, and love. A photo of my parents' six children shows her standing behind me with a hand of my shoulder. Our sibling love aged well. She remained a quiet but powerful influence on my life and work as a Jesuit priest and professor, built around thirty-three years of teaching theology at the Gregorian University (Rome).

What Maev contributed to my story shines through the 69 letters I wrote to her from 1978 to 2017—mainly from my home base in Rome. When that surviving correspondence began, she was the head of what became the Department of Anthropology and Sociology at the University of Papua New Guinea. On retirement in 1989 she returned to Australia and chose to live in Canberra. There she could have richer contacts with Papua New Guinea and the rest of Melanesia. After the 1990s, we met more often, and did not need to write regularly to each other. She visited our older sisters in Melbourne, Moira Peters and Dympna Coleman; they shared with her the letters I wrote to them. After 1999, only two letters (one from 2006 and the other from 2017) have survived that were specifically written to Maev.

Apart from illuminating the sibling relationship of Maev and myself, these letters answer a question frequently raised by those who visit Rome. What goes on behind the walls of the church institutions of education that are spread around the city? The letters provide fresh insights into life at the Gregorian University, founded in 1551 and still a university of the nations.

I thank my nephew Nicholas Coleman for supplying the

photographs reproduced in this book. The original texts of the letters reproduced in this volume are preserved in the archives of the Australian Jesuit Province (Hawthorn, Victoria). My thanks also go out to another nephew Les Coleman, who made available the appendix (a brief biography of Maev) and the chronology (see below).

During a long and fascinating life, Maev showed herself a person 'for others', constantly concerned to promote the rights and wellbeing of everyone, no matter who they were.[1] The letters I wrote to her persistently reflect the impact of her wise love on me, her younger brother Gerald. May she rest in peace and rise in glory.

Jesuit Theological College, 12 February 2023.

1 For a full account of her life, see Maev O'Collins as told to her nephew Les Coleman, *Last of the Lands We Know* (Brisbane: Connor Court Publications, 2013).

At ‘Rock Lodge’, Frank and Joan O’Collins with sons Jim (left), Glynn (right), and Gerald (standing) and daughters Dympna (left) and Moira (right); Maev was away but sent a photo to be added on the left: 1949.

Chronology

16 June 1929, born Brighton (Melbourne), Australia

1947–50, studies at the University of Melbourne, leading to BA

1951 studies at the University of Sydney, leading to a Graduate Diploma in Social Studies

1952–67 social worker with Catholic Social Services (later Catholic Family Welfare Bureau), Melbourne

1967 received a scholarship awarded by the American Association of University Women to study in the USA

1967–71 studies at Columbia University, New York

1969–70 taught Master's course ('Social Processes') at Hunter College, New York

1972 Doctorate in Social Welfare, Columbia University

1972 at the University of Papua New Guinea (Port Moresby), founded the Department of Social Work, later the Department of Anthropology and Sociology, of which she became professor and head in 1979

1987 awarded an MBE (Member of the Order of the British Empire) by the government of Papua New Guinea

1989 retired as professor emerita of the University of Papua New Guinea

1989 settled in Canberra as Honorary Visiting Fellow of the Australian National University

2002 published *Norfolk Island and the Commonwealth of Australia*: *An Uneasy Relationship* (Canberra: Pandanus Press)

2013 with Les Coleman wrote her autobiography *Last of the Lands We Know* (Brisbane: Connor Court Publishing).

3 July 2021 died at her home in Canberra.

Contents

Illustrations

1

Letters from 5 March 1978 to 5 January 1986

This letter mentions Tony Ruhan, an Australian Jesuit who spent some time as Maev's colleague at the University of Papua Guinea (Port Moresby), Peter Carnley who was in Rome representing the Anglican Communion and would in 1981 be appointed Anglican Archbishop of Perth (Western Australia), Moira and Marion Peters (my eldest sister and her eldest daughter), Karl Holzbauer (a Jesuit friend who was Caritas CEO in Nürnberg), and Joe Tagg III (an American seminarian from the South).

5 March 1978, Gregorian University.

My dear Maev, Tony Ruhan arrived last night, but I haven't seen him yet, as I am out on retreat [eight days of silence and prayer] in a convent on the via Cassia. In an area called 'Nero's Tomb', I am enjoying the peace and quiet, and the chance to pray.

The day I went out on retreat, I thought it was about time to escape. Starting after breakfast came an Indian (wanting help to get funds for his final year of doctoral research), a Canadian I am writing a book with [René Latourelle as co-editor of *Problems and Perspectives of Fundamental Theology*], an Irishman about to start a thesis with me, an American struggling through his master's thesis, and then an Australian bishop wanting to straighten out some of his colleagues. That took me through till after midday. It seemed like high time to get away.

Peter Carnley enjoyed his three weeks in Rome, which included a circus at the papal audience (yes, doing their thing: juggling, brass band, tumbling, pretty girls, clowns etc.) and a nice tussle with the Holy Office. The lads there, or at least their episcopal [surely cardinal?] chief, Franjo Seper, defended the position that the document against the ordination of women [*Inter Insigniores* of 1976] was 'the truth', and yet they declined to call it 'irreformable'. Ho, ho!

The PNG [Papua New Guinean] calendar looks splendid on my bookcase. Thank you for that. I push off for Nürnberg on 20 March—a kind of R & R with a couple of old Jesuit friends. Reading, writing, and some pastoral work. Moira and Marion are going to make their trek there, although I suspect we might compromise and meet in Munich. A pity if they don't come to Nürnberg as Karl Holzbauer will give them royal treatment when they do. [They came and were royally received.]

Joe Tagg will be priested soon. I borrowed his copy of *The Thorn Birds*, which I must return. [Joseph Tagg III, himself a lawyer, belonged to a family of pickle packers, who won an American show named, I think, 'What's your game?']

12 October 1978, Gregorian University.

My dear Maev, A friend is flying out to Australia in a day or so; hence this letter. Thanks for the books and the money for the Dean of Pembroke College, Cambridge. At the Gregorian, that edition of the *Summa Theologiae* will be much appreciated and long remain the standard work. [I referred to the gift of all 61 volumes of the translation prepared by Thomas Gilby, OP, and others.]

Epoca, a glossy weekly from Milan, carried much of what I said to Desmond O'Grady over the phone. The new rector here, Carlo Martini, liked the piece—which cheered me greatly, as I am never sure of the ins and outs of Italian church politics, even when you want to say nice things about a lovely pope who has just died [John Paul

I]. Someone carried a copy off to Posey [the wife of my brother Jim] in Melbourne. You can try out your Italian, or rather sample my Italian.

The cardinals better elect a successor to John Paul by Sunday or Monday. Otherwise when I give my first class on Tuesday, I won't have a soul there. Watch Cardinal Giovanni Benelli! The sense around town seems to be that you need a man with a gigantic and proven capacity to handle the work on Vatican Hill. Or is the choice between a loving, charismatic, communicative person who can't take the stress [another John Paul I] and an efficient bureaucrat? At any rate it seems clear that the cardinals may shift their criteria this time. I hope they will realize they picked a winner and look again for a good pastor. To hell with the work! The Vatican would be far better off, if it was all scaled down and the dioceses could handle their own affairs. Parkinson's Law operates like fury within the Vatican, or probably several of Parkinson's laws.

I am off to have a pizza with Dennis Sheehan. I am sure he would send his love to you all if he knew I was writing this letter. [Dennis was an American priest living and working in Rome.]

The Germans and Austrians got ordained this week in San Ignazio—all seven of them. A tremendous choir from Münster cathedral. A full church with the Germans lifting the roof off. It all acts like a great cathedral for me. The Hungarian primate (a cardinal) did the ceremony and preached at length, starting from the Turkish occupation of Hungary and ending with Pope John Paul saying the rosary. [Allegedly John Paul I died saying the rosary.] But his sermon fell short of the length of yesterday's first Mass of one of my students, or rather the length of the sermon preached by the lad's parish priest. A good forty minutes. Or rather a bad forty minutes. Great sincerity but endless repetition of the theme: "Trust Jesus and he will look after you." I agree thoroughly, but after forty minutes doubts were beginning to slip in. Was the parish priest protesting too much? Did he himself have secret doubts? Was he worried that Gerhard Maria Wagner had ever have been ordained?[2]

To get myself into shape for the first semester and the papal conclave, I am going off to Frascati for lunch on Saturday—with three Irish students.

Love to all and keep battling on with life. You are GREAT. But I still would love to see you settled into Glynneath [her house in Frankston, outside Melbourne]. Do I need

2 On 31 January 2009, Pope Benedict XVI appointed Wagner an auxiliary bishop of Linz, Austria. But two weeks later Wagner himself requested that the appointment be withdrawn. It had already generated strong opposition, prompted by his extreme views (e.g. that the Harry Potter novels revealed Satanism and that the sins of the people of New Orleans had caused hurricane Katrina).

a security picture, "Maev is in Glynneath, and all's well with the world"? Con amore, Gerald.

[This letter refers to my nephews, Stewart and James Peters, to an Italian friend Mimi Sbisà, and to Bishop Kennedy, an auxiliary of the Archdiocese of Adelaide, South Australia.]

12 November 1978, Gregorian.

My dear Maev,

I am just waiting for a call from Stewart, who is flying in from Tel Aviv. Then we have to decide who does the heroic act and meets James at the airport at 5.30 a.m. tomorrow morning. [Stewart did.]

Bishop Phil Kennedy carried home that letter you received from me. Phil flew out of Rome the very hour Pope John Paul died. By the way, Count Leo Ceschi's godson, Leo Maasburg, is in my first-year class (of 160). An added incentive to get myself up to Vicenza [where Ceschi lived] one day.

The editors of that Italian monthly *Ad Gentes* [on missionary activity] have translated your article into Italian, like it *very* much, and are ravenous for a little more. They want to make it a star feature. Could you face doing about seven to eight typed pages on the Church (or rather the Churches), their arrival in the country [Papua

New Guinea], the way the people received the message, and the place of the Churches in the development of the country? (I take it the magazine would like more emphasis on the Roman Catholic Church, but would not want the other Churches to be ignored.) And then three to four pages on the style of life, the culture, art, social order, economic character and structure of Papua New Guinea? That sounds as if you would need to write hundreds of pages! However, they only want three to four pages. I hope this won't be a bother to you. But Assunta Ozzi and the others liked your article greatly and want to expand it with the additions indicated. There is no great rush, incidentally.

I hope those wretched people on the appointments committee at Melbourne University realize the error of their ways, and rethink matters to the point of inviting you. How foolish can people be! [Equipped with a doctorate from Columbia University, New York, with teaching experience at Hunter College, New York and with some years leading a department at the University of Papua New Guinea, Maev had applied to become head of social studies at Melbourne University. The committee, chaired by Eric D'Arcy, later the Archbishop of Hobart (Tasmania), turned her down: "a strong candidate but has not yet headed a department at a major university." This "Catch 22" reasoning would mean that no one could ever become head of such a department!]

Dimension Books is much better at mailing books when I ask them to do so. *A Month with Jesus* arrived promptly out in Australia. Paulist Press who have published *The Second Journey* are rather remiss about such matters. Hence no copies have yet hit Australia for the family or for the shops.

I gave Mimi Sbisà a call, and she seemed enthusiastic about Stewart and me (plus James, I suppose) coming up to Castel Gandolfo next week.

Does Moira have Genevieve Albers' address in Seattle? I hope I am spelling her name right. When I saw her in Seattle last year, she spoke about coming to Rome. With a new pope, I might encourage her to do so. She just might think that the Gregorian was worth putting some money into, instead of giving it all to Seattle University. The Greg still staggers along in the red. I used to think the Vatican might terminate my stay here. But it might be the bailiffs. Anyway, if you can dig her address out of Moira's book, I would be glad to have it—for the aforesaid intention. [Albers, a friend of my sister Moira, was heir to the Carnation Company, acquired in 1984 by Nestlé.] Much love, Gerald. [After staying in St John's College, University of Queensland, Brisbane, with Peter and Ann Carnley, I had just arrived at St Joseph's

Seminary (Mangalore). A lecture tour of India would take me to Bangalore and back to Bombay before I returned to face the new academic year in Rome. Maev's dear friend and a member of the National Parliament of Papua New Guinea (1977–87), Nahau Rooney, had been gaoled for contempt after she intervened with the Director of Public Prosecutions on Manus Island but quickly released. Legal proceedings still continued.]

6 September 1979, Mangalore.

My dear Maev, I do hope that the outcome of the Rooney case brought peace and reconciliation. When I left the Carnleys and Brisbane last Friday, one of the papers reported that a decision would be reached that day. But, of course, it has been impossible to have any news [from Papua New Guinea] here in India.

When I reached Bombay at 6 a.m. on Saturday, it was a relief to see my suitcase (looking rather moist in the humid heat) come bobbing along the belt with the rest of the luggage. It seemed like a miracle of human cooperation—that I could leave the case with Ansett in Brisbane at 1 p.m., join the Qantas flight in Sydney at 5.30 p.m., and recover the case early next morning in Bombay.

After a good morning's sleep I did a bit of sightseeing in the afternoon: first, up to Mount Mary, a Portuguese church with a lovely statue of Our Lady high above the main altar. People were streaming up there for the novena devotions at 5 p.m. During the novena that leads up to the feast of Our Lady's nativity, every Catholic family in Bombay will try to visit that church. For a rupee I bought a candle, asked Our Lady to bless these weeks in India, and added my candle to the pile in front of the high altar.

As I made my way back to the Church of Our Lady of Victories where I was staying, parties of Hindus were carrying gaudy statues of an elephant god down to the shore. According to legend, he saved his mother from rape but in the process had his nose sliced off. He was rewarded (by other gods?) by having an elephant's trunk attached to his mutilated face. The Hindus dunk the statues in the water and then carry home the remains. I saw a few carrying platters with little mounts of mud on them—relics of the elephant god to be preserved for the coming year.

On Sunday I flew to Mangalore in an old Anson, and at times clutched the arm rest for dear life, as there was only half a safety belt on my seat. Priests, sisters, seminarians, and lay people have given me an overwhelming welcome here. It will make it hard to leave Mangalore.

Much love, Gerald.

[Uncle Jim (James Patrick O'Collins) had been bishop of Geraldton (Western Australia) before becoming bishop of Ballarat (Victoria). An Australian journalist and writer, Desmond O'Grady lived in Rome until his death in 2021 and became a treasured friend of mine.]

26 March 1980, Gregorian University.

My dear Maev, I am sitting here waiting to see what alternate arrangements for a flight to London the travel agent comes up with, now that Sudan Airways have cancelled today's flight to London I was on. I hope to be over in the UK for two weeks, leading the Holy Week ceremonies, having a break etc. So let's see what comes up. At this point I hardly feel like stopping around in Rome till Saturday.

The old ecclesiastical tailors, Gammarelli, have just finished a soutane for Uncle Jim. When Moira [our eldest sister] pointed out he needed a new one for the May celebration [of fifty years a bishop], he said that Gammarelli would still have his measurements. And sure enough, there was his card, with his last purchase being in 1965 at the end of the Second Vatican Council. One of the tailors remembered meeting Uncle Jim that year not only in the shop but also in the Rome zoological gardens. The tailor had his children with him, and Uncle Jim gave them a blessing. The moral? Your blessings are remembered after you?

Paulist Press kindly accepted for publication my *Fundamental Theology* (around 430 pages of ms) and promise to have it out around October. In the final pages I quote your inaugural [lecture] and apply what you say in the last lines to the situation of Gregorian professors. I thought it went well—the transfer of sentiments. So I hope you will be 'd'accordo [in agreement]'. I dated the introduction to Uncle Gerald's birthday in May. [He was a Columban missionary for many years in China.]

Do you remember talking to me about a book (his diaries?) by a Russian explorer who was in Melanesia in the last century? Would it be awfully expensive to send Desmond O'Grady a copy—surface mail? He was interested in it, maybe as a basis for a story, when I spoke to him some months ago. (I've seen him often since, but around Christmas we were talking about Melanesia.) Are there relatives of the Russian in Sydney? I have a vague memory of your telling me that. Any information would be welcome. Desmond's address is: via Bartolomeo 77, 00191 Roma, Italy.

I hope the change of government [in PNG] has not been too traumatic. We get so little news here, beyond the simple fact that it has changed. I won't be going to the Society of the Divine Word at Nemi until after Easter, and so have not had news via those on the course who come from PNG.

Have a great Easter. Much love, Gerald.

[I mentioned a visit by Davis and Jean McCaughey; he was currently governor of the State of Victoria. Jim and Jackie McDonald lived in New Jersey, and had become close friends of Maev during her time of study in New York.]

9 June 1980, Gregorian University.

My dear Maev, A very happy birthday next Monday; I hope you have someone suitable to celebrate it with. Thank you for your paper on avoiding obfuscation. The more I read by you, the more I see the resemblance between your existence there and mine here. Did I tell you that I quoted a paragraph from your inaugural lecture at the end of my book *Fundamental Theology* (to appear next October or so in both English and Italian), and then applied what you said to my own work on the banks of the Tiber?

There was a pleasant reception for Joan Sutherland at the Australian Ambassador's home. She has been highly acclaimed in London and here [in Rome] for her Lucretia Borgia role. When I met her, I remarked: 'the Pope sends his apologies for being out of town.' He was in Paris at the time. She laughed and said: 'he's a much busier person than I am.' I thought she might have observed the fact that she was playing the part of a pope's daughter!

Today the McCaugheys came to dinner at the Gregorian, and were asking after you with much affection, especially Jean. I was probably pushing my luck having them to dine with the [Jesuit] community. But the old boys, I must admit, are changing somewhat. Abigail McCarthy dined with us a few weeks back, as one of a party of North American benefactors of our international houses in Rome. She is Senator Eugene McCarthy's ex-wife. A lovely, gentle person, she came along to a graduate seminar of mine in the afternoon. I hope she has a positive impression of everything, since she is writing, or perhaps has already written an article on Jesuits for the *Washington Post.* The one point she really insisted on was the need for priests to be thoroughly professional in what they take on.

Jim McDonald invited me out to dinner a fortnight ago. He had his left eye removed for a tumour, and is in remarkably good spirits about it. He wears a black patch and, yes, has a Moshe Dayan [defence minister of Israel] look. I will stay with them one night next week on my way through New York. Jim is back at work, can drive etc., and it seems that they caught the tumour in time. Maybe Jackie has already written to you about all this.

Last week I went out to our villa in Frascati, and flopped. It has been an exhausting second semester, especially with all the extra things which have come up. This summer I am committed to some teaching in San Francisco and then in Kyoto. I hope it won't be too disappointing if I don't come to PNG. Several reasons [for this]: the main two are the question of time and the need to husband energies a bit. It would be an awful rush to get down [to PNG] and then back to Europe. And I suppose too that some of the family in Australia would find it odd if I went to PNG but not on to Melbourne. I hope you understand. In mid-1981, I will get out Rome for a good slice of time. If I don't see you in Melbourne, I will head up to PNG.

Much love, Gerald.

[My brother Jim, wife Posey, two children, and Posey's sister Kate with her family spent the Christmas of 1980 with me in Rome.]

10 January 1981, Gregorian University.

My dear Maev, Happy days. and thanks for the cards from Fiji. By the way, Mimi [Sbisà] from Castel Gandolfo sends her best wishes. I overheard her describing you to some friends as 'simpaticissima'. So there. Plans are to spend the very end of July and August [1981] in or about Melbourne.

It was a lovely visit from Jim, Posey, James, Tori [Victoria], Kate etc. I hated to see them go.

Love, Gerald,

[John and Judy Brophy were friends from Sydney; Jim and Bill McCarthy were cousins from Melbourne, and Frances the wife of Jim.]

10 October 1980, Gregorian University.

My dear Maev, Thanks for the information on 'ad hoc' encounters and letter. Rome is full of 'ad hoc stuff'. Since I returned two weeks ago, visitors from the USA, Germany, Australia, and Norway have been running at the rate of one or more a day. It has meant that I haven't had too much time with John and Judy or with the McCarthys.

Sooner or later copies of the July/August number of *Ad Gentes*, the missionary magazine that asked you for the article on PNG, will reach you. They dug out from somewhere in Rome the worst photos (from your point of view) and added some horrendous headings. But otherwise you may be pleased. I did try to tell one Italian that, despite the photo of the chap with a human skull, 'they are not cannibals'. But he replied with a smile: 'But I think they are.' The triumph of will over facts!

Hans Küng was pretty chippy when I had a drink with him in Germany en route back here [Rome]. He retains his ecumenical institute, depends directly on the president of Tübingen university, is no longer a member of the Catholic theological faculty (& hence doesn't examine students in that faculty), gives open lectures, and is off to the States for a fortnight next month. He (and others) have prepared an open letter to the Pope [John Paul II] for the Pope's visit to Germany next month. I forgot to check the dates of the papal visit and Küng's trip to the USA. It may be that HK will be out of the country for the papal visit. I told HK that he should try to have supper with the pontiff. 'But he never has critical people to meals', he replied. 'How do you know?', I asked him. 'Anyway', I added, 'never ventured, never won'.

I stopped overnight with the Noltes [Josef and Ingrid, friends who lived just outside Tübingen]. They were glad to have news of you and send their very best wishes. They have got to know the Harbisons [cousins of mine from Dublin]; Janet [a first rate harpist] was over to perform at a function in Tübingen which Josef arranged. Next summer the Noltes will very likely spend some time in Kerry [southern Ireland] at the holiday home, which Jock [Harbison] bought years ago.

Did I tell you that I finished my last magnum opus in theology (over 300 pages of *Fundamental Theology*) with an extract from your inaugural lecture, adding that I thought it bore somewhat on my position as an expatriate theologian in Italy?

Much love, Gerald.

[This letter mentions Sir James and Lady Shirley Gobbo; a high court judge, Jim was to become a governor of the State of Victoria. Alex and Marjory Lynch were friends from Melbourne. I would write an obituary of Alex for the Melbourne *Age*.]

20 May 1981, Gregorian University.

My dear Maev, Thank you very much for your letter, birthday card, and gift, Moira will be there [in Rome] for the 2nd, with the Gobbos and the Lynches. So I will not be lonely. A very happy birthday to your dear self on the 16th. I hope there are some good folks around to celebrate it with.

We have just been through an extraordinary week. After the Pope was shot on 13 May, they had him on the operating table in forty minutes or a little less. Back in St Peter's Square, some young people brought a photo of him and put it on the spot where the shooting took place and laid some red roses alongside. It is just a few yards, of course, from where St Peter was crucified and buried. When the Pope revived after the five and a half hour operation, he thanked the doctors, the nurses, and old Alessandro Pertini (the Italian President who stayed in the hospital the whole time and has continued to show enormous concern). Then the Pope asked how the two women shot with him were getting on.

Last Sunday, just four days after the assassination attempt, the pope did a tape that was broadcast in St Peter's Square at midday: forgiving his assassin, praying for the two persons wounded with him, and thanking everyone for their prayers and sympathy. People wept in the square, covered their faces with their hands, or knelt to pray when they heard JP II's voice coming over the loudspeakers. Obviously he was still in pain, breathing heavily, speaking slowly and with less power, but it was the same firm, affectionate voice.

The group of foreign medical experts, who came to check on the Pope's condition, in their signed statement yesterday concurred with their Italian colleagues, adding that he must take a long rest. I wonder whether the Vatican invited the foreigners to try to put more pressure on the Pope to take it easy when he gets out of hospital.

I leave for the States around 20 June, come back briefly to the Gregorian 20/21 July, and then out to Australia (essentially Melbourne) 23 July until the end of August. I really hope we can meet up during those weeks. There is a little bit of help that I am expected to give to a priest who will be doing some fund-raising for the Gregorian. But otherwise I don't have much on.

Much love, Gerald.

[The letter mentions the son and daughter-in-law of John and Judy Brophy (see letter of 10 October 1980), Gerard and Jill Brophy. Gerard spent a couple of years studying music and musical composition in Italy. Their landlord in Rome, Signor Tofanelli, had apparently clashed with Maev, or vice versa.]

25 February 1982, Gregorian University.

My dear Maev, Thanks for the letter and the review [of *Fundamental Theology*] from *The Catholic Herald.*[3] It was good and positive. In fact all the reviews bar one so far have been that way. The one exception came from an old friend, Maurice Wiles, whose version of Christian faith I couldn't share but whose practice I would be happy to follow. He is an extraordinarily kind person, and a couple of years ago cared in a wonderful way for a young priest [James Lyons] from Australia, who wrote a doctorate with him and died of cancer just before finishing it. Maurice put the last chapter together (from

3 Perhaps I meant *The Catholic Weekly*, published in Sydney and so readily accessible to Maev. It is hard to imagine her coming across any review in *The Catholic Herald*, a London-based weekly paper.

the student's notes and final conversations with him), had it accepted by Oxford University, saw the degree awarded posthumously, and now has had the thesis published.

My address in Germany (18 March to around 24 May) is: bei Holzbauer, Caritas-Pirckheimer-Haus, 85 Nürnberg, Königstrasse 64, West Germany.

A couple of weeks ago, I finished correcting the final proofs for the Italian translation of *Fundamental Theology* [Brescia: Queriniana, 1982]. Then I went off to make a retreat [eight days of silence and prayer] out at Grotta Ferrata in the Alban Hills. It snowed in Calabria and Sicily. It was an odd thing on 20 February to spot about 75 geese up about 1000 feet and heading *north* in a v-formation at about 30 miles an hour. If they thought it was spring already, they must like it cold. Or maybe their chief was leading them astray.

In a few minutes I have a round-table discussion with colleagues in fundamental theology and attendant students. The whole meeting may run for a couple of hours (10–12 a.m.). It is the first time we have tried something like this in fundamental theology. It is a kind of show of strength in the face of the larger groups specializing in dogmatic theology etc.

This afternoon around 50 or 60 non-Roman Catholics come for a couple of hours to discuss the true nature of human beings. They are down in Rome from an ecumenical institute in Bossey [Switzerland].

Sunday evening I will have a pizza with Gerard and Jill Brophy (and maybe her sister, if she is back from Florence). They are still at Tofanelli's. I met the old boy the other night. He doesn't seem too bad. You must have done something to arouse him.

Much love, Gerald.

[This letter mentions an Irish friend, Aideen Archbold who lived for years in Rome, and Count Leo Ceschi, an Italian business man and friend of my family, whose son Alex married an Australian lady in Vicenza. Aideen worked for a time with Vatican Radio, to which I had helped send some interviews of Maev.]

20 April 1982, Caritas Pirckheimer Haus, Nürnberg.

Dear Maev, Thanks for your letter which reached me here in the good old *Vaterland*. Just before I left Rome, I phoned Aideen to wish her a happy St Patrick's Day, but forgot to ask her about the taped interviews [from Maev in Papua New Guinea]. By the way [apropos of the Celtic tribes], don't believe that story about the sacred geese warning the Romans that the Celts would stage a night attack. The Celts took Rome! No mistake about it, but the Romans made up that pious story to cover up a sad episode in their history. It's significant that the Romans never tried to cross the Irish Sea. They did defeat those decadent [!] French Gauls, but not the real thing or real things guarding the Western Approaches.

Germany just had its first 'Retortenbaby' (conceived in vitro), born just up the road in a hospital at Erlangen. His name is Oliver [and made me think of Oliver Twist]. Incidentally, on German TV last week there was a program on male infertility—very 'clinical', as Mother would have said, and in perfect taste, the taste being slightly tarnished only by a urologist fitting in some kind of plumber-talk you get from Jim [our surgeon brother]. All was fiercely scientific, except when one of the serious young doctors was asked about age: 'No problem', he said with utter sincerity, 'look at [ancient] Abraham and others in the Old Testament,'

Here in Nuremberg I have been reading, writing, renewing my German, enjoying some excellent concerts, rejoicing in the fact that the phone in my room never rings, and adjusting to the fact that in four weeks I must get on the road back to Rome. I will stop with the Noltes in Tübingen, and help with Alex Ceschi's wedding in Vicenza.

Most Sundays I am in Merrell Barracks, a US army base

just outside town. Last Sunday an altar girl Patricia, aged nine, confided that she was tired of being alone when serving Mass for me Sunday after Sunday, and yet concerned that back in the States there is now a freeze on altar girls in many parishes. 'Patricia', [I said], 'you cross that line when you go home in two years time. Right now, can't you get Justin, Matthew, and the other boy to come and serve?' I await developments next Sunday. It was Cardinal James Knox [an Australian] from his Roman office who told the clergy around the world that altar girls were out. And now you see what he is doing to a nine-year-old in a former SS barracks outside Nürnberg.

I hope that I will write again in time for 16 June. If not, a very happy birthday then. Much love, Gerald.

6 June 1982, Gregorian University.

My dear Maev, Thank you for the birthday telegram, and a very happy birthday to your dear self on the 16th. By the way, your taped interviews with the Vatican Radio got used in three programs: overseas service, English-speaking broadcasts for Africa, and something that went out to India. Apparently there is a tiny cheque somewhere in the pipeline heading towards me; no word on tapes.

On 23 May after a farewell Mass in the Merrell Barracks

in Nürnberg, I took the train to Stuttgart, had afternoon tea with Gerhard and Barbara Mattes [friends from the University of Tübingen], a drink with a friend Bernd [Stappert, a journalist] who seems to be starving himself to death, and then on by a 8 p.m. train to Tübingen and a couple of days with the Noltes in Hirschau [a village just out of Tübingen]. I have never seen the meadows look lovelier; Tübingen was its splendid, usual self. I dropped around to Küng's institute, but he wasn't in his office. As time was short, I didn't call on him in his home up the hill. He is running a series of lectures on non-Christian religions, and next week opens a research program (generously funded by some foundation) on women in the early Church. Josef & Ingrid Nolte were asking after you with great affection.

Via Zürich I travelled to Geneva to stop a day with Richard Incledon, who used to be the Roman Catholic chaplain at Cambridge University and now is parish priest for the English-speaking Catholics in Geneva. Just across the landing from his apartment is Carl Gustav Jung's nephew. After Geneva, I went via Milan to Vicenza and the wedding of Alex Ceschi. A Franciscan did the wedding in a thousand-year-old, Romanesque church, and I added some prayers and a brief homily in English.

After a couple of busy weeks in Rome, I fly to the United States on 11 June; I will be c/o Jesuit Community,

Gonzaga University, Spokane, Washington 99258, USA, 11 June until 23 July. Then ten days or so in Washington, New York, and Wyckoff (New Jersey, where Jim and Jackie McDonald lived), and to London around 2 August. Finally, I return to Rome at the end of the month.

Tomorrow—whoops today—I'm having lunch with Gerard and Jill Brophy.

Much love, Gerald,

8 July 1982, Gonzaga University, Spokane.

My dear Maev, fantastic news from Manus [Island]. I am dying to hear the final result [of the legal proceedings involving her friend Nahau Rooney]. Just to keep the pot boiling, here is a cutting from the *New York Times.* Was some expatriate pulling the leg of those American women? In case you want to correct the paper, especially on the cannibalism bit, here is the address: *New York Times*, 229 West 43rd Street, New York, NY 10036, USA.

I teach here until 23 July, then visit the various bodies out East—Marion [Peters, a niece in Washington], Joanna [Peters] & Bob [a niece and her husband in New York], and, finally, the McDonalds [friends in New Jersey]. I will be with them the weekend of 31 July/2 August. I then fly to Amsterdam to visit an old theologian [Piet

Smulders, SJ], to London, to lecture in Durham, and then back to Rome at the end of August.

Bing Crosby studied at this university where I am lecturing [Gonzaga]. Bob Hope spoke at the commencement shortly after Crosby's death. Was Dorothy Lamour invited? I'll ask and let you know. [Lamour appeared with Crosby and Hope in a series of 'road' films: for instance, *The Road to Morocco* and *The Road to Zanzibar.*]

In haste but with much love, Gerald.

PS It is interesting to notice how the theme of cannibalism [raised by *Ad Gentes*; see letter of 10 October 1980] has made me introduce words like 'pot', 'boiling', and 'bodies'—unintentionally, I assure you.

[The letter mentions my oldest nephew and his wife, Stewart and Nola Peters, and Giorgio Barzilai, who had been one of the young Italian scientists working in Rome at the time of Enrico Fermi, who shifted to the USA and helped develop the atomic bomb.]

30 September 1982, Gregorian University.

My dear Maev, Thanks very much for the letter of 23 June, the paper, and earlier the telegram for my birthday. After spending mid-June until 2 August in the USA (mostly teaching [for a summer program), a week of sightseeing and work in a Vatican II archive in Amsterdam [with Piet Smulders, SJ], and three weeks in England. I returned to Rome a month ago.

In London, incidentally, John Ellison [married to my cousin Monica] was running a front-page piece in the *Daily Express* on electric boxes for putting dogs down. The RSPCA approve of dogs taking the long walk that way, but thousands of Brits feel otherwise. So John put on the front page the photographs of executions at dawn in the Battersea dog home.

In England I took the youngest Ellison [Charlotte] up to Cambridge for day, but she may defect to the other place. She comes up for Oxbridge exams & A levels in May or so 1983. To compensate I took the youngest Mason girl, Mimi, up to Oxford. [Kate Mason was the older sister of my sister-in-law Posey, and lived with her three daughters in London.] Mimi is only thirteen, but I thought it no harm sowing the idea in her mind. We lunched with some friends of mine, Peter and Margaret Hebblethwaite. Halfway through the meal, the baby (Benedict) was feeling a bit peckish. So—on the principle of equal rights for everyone?—Margaret started breast-feeding at the table. I thought Mimi was going to faint at the sight of milk.

Stewart and Nola spent a good week here. We had a pre-lunch drink one Sunday with that Spanish brother-infirmarian, José Luis Ruiz, SJ, who was delightedly showing me the card you had sent him. Afterwards, thanks to Moira and Dympna [their gift], we had lunch with Gerard and Jill Brophy (plus Chiara Francesca, just thirteen days old). Next Wednesday I expect to baptize Chiara in St Peter's Basilica—with John and Judy [Brophy, the grandparents] in attendance. Aideen [see letter of 20 April 1982 above] is joining us afterwards for a celebration. Talking of celebrations, she gave a supper for Stewart and Nola which took almost a week to recover from.

For Stewart, the highlight [of this visit] was meeting old Giorgio [Barzilai], a retired professor from the University of Rome. He had worked on radar jamming during World War II—in Sicily against the British navy around Malta. When Italy changed sides, Giorgio found himself or got himself onto the right side of the front and was flown off to London for talks with British intelligence. They hugged him, when quite incidentally he disclosed that his operation had the code name Caruso. [Up to that point] they imagined it was something to do with the development of the atomic bomb in Germany and were spending time chasing a totally false lead. Giorgio called the operation 'Caruso', because old Caruso used to shout every now and then, and Giorgio's jamming procedure involved booming now and then.

Much love, Gerald.

24 October 1982, Gregorian University.

My dear Maev, thank you very much for the copy of *Bikmaus* and your paper, 'Small is still beautiful'. At our opening Mass in the Church of San Ignazio, Gregorian staff and students heard pidgin [with English the official language of Papua New Guinea] for the first time: an MSC [Missionary of the Sacred Heart] read one of the prayers of the faithful in that language.

A friend of Mimi Sbisà's, Giorgio Barzilai, may be visiting PNG. A seventy-year old retired professor of physics, he is fond of wandering off to warmer climes during the winter and may be headed your way. He was very impressed by your article, but I warned him you were not responsible for the photographs or title. (I am referring to the piece in Italian in *Ad Gentes*.) If you want more information on Giorgio, ask Stewart Peters who spent half a day with him.

John and Judy Brophy left last Thursday, after coming for the baptism of Chiara Francesca (done by myself in the parish church of the Vatican, Saint Anna's). Gerard and Jill [Brophy] turn up with the baby on Sundays for the eleven o'clock concelebration in the Church of the Gesù. I get a special thrill from seeing 'my' baby parked in a pram on the side of the aisle—across from the tomb of Saint Ignatius, on the one side, and the right arm of

St Francis, on the other. Chiara is only the 5th or 6th child I have baptized. It is an even 'better' Mass these days at eleven a.m.: larger choir, more concelebrants, a good crowd of people etc. [Only later did I learn that one of those people was Ennio Morricone, who composed much memorable music for films.]

Over lunch yesterday an old Spanish canon lawyer (who also works for a Vatican office) told me that he had just finished six weeks' work on a candidate for beatification and been paid his 100,000 lire ($70 US). 'The result?', I asked. 'Bocciato (failed)', he said. Then yesterday evening I went to the North American College for the Eucharist at which the second-year theologians became lectors. As we lined up in the corridor, I found myself next to another (much younger) priest, an American who also works in that office for the causes of 'santi' and 'beati' (saints and blesseds). I asked: 'How is Mother Mary McKillop's cause getting along?' 'I spent last week on her', he told me, but not a flicker of an eyelid betrayed the nature of his judgement. 'Give her a chance', I said. The old Spaniard [Ramón Bidagor], incidentally, had assured me: 'I don't touch anything after the 18th century.'

In a few minutes I am off to a reception for group of Anglican clergy who have spent two weeks in Rome. On Friday I talked to them on theological education in Rome. Canon Burgess Carr I had met in Ghana eight years ago. He is an historian who now teaches at Yale. In those days he was the influential general secretary of the African Council of Churches.

Much love, Gerald.

2 January 1983, Gregorian University.

My dear Maev, In a few minutes I am off to the [Church of the] Gesù to preach on the Magi (were they Melanesians?), and meet Gerard, Jill and Chiara Brophy. I tell the Italians that the Magi were genuine Australians and that they really came from the Far East.

On New Year's Eve I was at Maria Franca Lamaro's, but without you things were dull. You won't believe this, but over dinner all of us hardly finished one bottle of wine. At midnight we had to hold burning sparklers on the balcony. To drive away evil spirits? The French, or the ones I knew in Paris, would go through the kitchen and house banging saucepans to bring about the same happy effect. So a bit of noise and fire does the trick.

I think I mentioned Giorgio, that retired professor who plans a trip to Papua New Guinea. On New Year's Eve he asked me to check three things with you, if you don't mind. When is the wet weather in PNG? In Port Moresby can he stay near a cheerful beach? (Getting into the sun on a tropical beach seems one of the objects of his tour.) What kind of prices should he expect in hotels in Port Moresby or elsewhere? If you could get me an answer fairly soon, Giorgio would be grateful. He has become a good pal of mine, and really made a hit with Stewart and Nola [Peters]. He had them out to a party (his youngest's birthday) the night before they left Rome. His wife, English and Catholic, died 15 years ago or so. The two boys and the girl are now grown up.

Betty Kilham Roberts [a solicitor who ran the Society of Authors] was asking after you with much affection. I saw her at the Dorias' carol party.

Remember the vice-rector of the English College who complained last year about the Christmas tree in the Piazza Venezia? He didn't come to the carol party this time. Did he want to avoid hurting his eyes through that tree flashing at him when he left for home in the College?

Much love, Gerald.

26 January 1984, Gregorian University.

My dear Maev, Thanks very much for the two letters (plus the Christmas card from Japan, which eventually made their way through the Italian postal service). Last Saturday we gave old Goethe another bash; this time the group met at the Beda [College]. Sister Mary Peter was down with the flu and couldn't attend. In answer to your question, yes, the evening went off with less strain. In fact, I have rarely enjoyed more the company of Sean O'Riordan [a Redemptorist], Martin [Molyneux, vice-rector of the Beda] etc. Sean was quoting German poetry and diction with resounding relish.

On the negative side, segregation will be practised tonight in connection with the Australia Day celebrations in Rome. Once again, with a squad of clerics and sisters, I have been invited to the reception at the home of the Chargé d'Affaires of the Australian Embassy to the Holy See. All the decent lay people like Desmond O'Grady have their own party at the Australian Embassy to the Italian Republic. We need affirmative action in defence of clerical rights to pick which party we desire to patronize

Maria Franca [Lamaro], and even more her children, were just delighted with the photos you sent. They wanted to thank you warmly for them. My guess is that what really pleased them was the fact that their father, Sergio, looked cheerful in your shots.

CBS [Columbia Broadcasting System] will be back shortly to take a few last scenes for their Easter Sunday evening TV program on the Gregorian. Did I tell you that, before the CBS team came to Rome, they had been filming in Lebanon. They had to wait for pauses in the bombing and shelling when they were doing an interview with a patriarch. Back in New York that segment kept inserting a click every now and then; they had heard nothing when taking the interview. 'The apartment was bugged', said the engineer. 'You couldn't hear anything, but the camera could.' But by whom? Israelis? Syrians? The perfidious French? The list of suspects is endless. I forgot to ask the team whether they got in touch with the patriarch to tell him that it might be a good idea to have his apartment debugged.

Was my November letter waiting for you in Canberra? Just one little thing I mentioned in it. If one of the family has a spare copy of my juvenile—no, early—work, *Man and his new Hopes*, I would be grateful for it. I remember that Mother had a few extra copies, which might be lying around somewhere. Here in Rome I don't have a copy for the Gregorian library, and students sometimes want to read it. An encouraging sign? All the library has is the Spanish translation.

Thank you again for a wonderful visit. It meant a great deal to me. Much love, Gerald. PS

12 April 1984, Gregorian University.

My dear Maev, Last night I was looking at two splendid slides of you in Canberra. Giorgio [Barzilai] had us all up to Marino [Laziale] for a welcome-back party and then turned on a slide show. The Canberra shots were definitely the best of the bunch.

I quite agree with your suggestion about the Pope returning [to Papua New Guinea] some of the Sepik [River] treasures stored in the basement at the Vatican. But I didn't again pass on the idea, as two or three ideas I passed on recently didn't evoke any kind of positive response. I am waiting for another Cardinal [James] Knox [an Australian] to come on the scene, as it was possible to do things through him. [I was thinking of how he helped at the 1973 Eucharistic Congress in Melbourne.]

April began with a cluster of visitors: Dick McBrien from the University of Notre Dame [South Bend, Indiana], who is always offering me a job there which I always turn down; Ted Yarnold from Campion Hall, Oxford; Jack Kennedy, the new rector of the English College; Gerard O'Keefe who was in the winning Xavier [College] crew of 1948—we re-rowed the race over some vino bianco; a Canadian (Anglican) priest with a thick accent (whose world revolves around Victorinus of Pannonia), Peter Hebblethwaite (who has just delivered his ms. on Pope

John XXIII to Geoffrey Chapman and warned me that I might appear in a novel his wife is writing about a Jesuit who becomes a hermit), [Professor] Owen Chadwick [of Cambridge], and one or two others.

The Dorias had an excellent luncheon party on Tuesday for Chadwick and his wife Ruth. Betty Kilham Roberts, asking after you with great affection, was there and Philip Caraman, a Jesuit who received Betty into the Catholic Church many years ago. It was touching to see the two of them meet for the first time thirty years or so later. When I asked Chadwick how long he would be staying in Rome, he said: 'I'll be returning to London next week.' He was too modest to say that he would be spending Holy Week with the Queen at Sandringham. As a regis professor of Cambridge and ordained Anglican priest, he gets to do the ceremonies and sermons for her and the royal family when they spend Easter at Sandringham.

March began with a death, the father of Emmanuela (the girl from Gucci's whose wedding I hope to celebrate later this year), and it ended with the death of Karl Rahner [a very great theologian] on 30 March. When we brought the body of E's father from the mortuary chapel to the parish church, we drove down the Via Appia Antica and past ancient Roman tombs before cutting to the left and across to the Casilina. I had an extraordinary sense of reliving the past—just as in Trier where you enter the cemetery and move beyond a late-Roman section and enter the Middle Ages and the modern times.

Giuseppe Lamaro is arriving in few minutes to drive me out to Ciampino and my charter flight to Gatwick. His mother, by the way, was trying to sell a villa on the Appia Antica, with catacomb attached. [Maria Franca Lamaro worked as an estate agent. Occasionally her work brought her into contact with legendary personalities like the actor Roberto Benigni.]

Much love, Gerald. PS Tell the Brophys how good it was to see them.

[This letter mentions Marion Peters, a niece married to Eric ('Rick') Brown, who lived in Washington, and a letter to a nephew Nicholas ('Nick') who decided to apply (successfully) to Cambridge University. I wanted to share in nominating Maev for the Albert Schweitzer Prize. My letter to Nick follows this letter.]

24 May 1984, Gregorian University.

My dear Maev, A very happy birthday on 16 June. I will be flying the Atlantic that day—Rome to Washington—and plan to lift a glass to you, the best of sisters and aunts, with Marion and Rick. If I can't celebrate the day with you, why not fly the Atlantic to make up?

Enclosed is a letter I sent to Nick, or rather a copy of the letter I sent him. I hope my advice was sound.

[I am] sorry to add an additional chore as your sabbatical moves to an end, but this year you are being proposed for the Albert Schweitzer Prize—under the heading of 'humanities'. There are in fact three prizes to be awarded in early 1985: for services under the headings of music, medicine, and humanities.

I enclose copies of the material I assembled in 1981. (1) Can you update the published and conference papers to 1984, adding works to come? (2) Could you update the curriculum vitae also? (3) Can you add in one or two PNGs [Papua New Guineans] as referees? Two preferably. If you want to change or add anything, do so at will. Please send the updated and corrected papers to me at: Jesuit Community, University of San Francisco, San Francisco, California 94117, USA.

It would be good if you could mail everything to me just as soon as possible. I will have the material typed professionally, and then send it all to a friend in Luxembourg who nominates for the Albert Schweitzer Prize and wants to nominate you this time. I regret to say that he was responsible for Mother Teresa winning an AS prize some years back. Maybe he wants to redress the balance now? [When Mother Teresa of Kolkata had visited Papua New Guinea, Maev spoke to her and against imposing on the local people the founding of yet another religious house in PNG.]

In haste but with much love, Gerald. PS I hope you are happy about the nomination; I am. Last time you listed Eric Perkins for the period 1953–67 and J. Kilage [a Papua New Guinean?] for 1972 and later. Please name the jobs of those who could be referees, PPS If you have one or two recent papers which illustrate how you reach out to different groups, they could be helpful.

20 May 1984, Gregorian University.

Dear Nick, First of all, congratulations on your truly excellent results in religious studies. It has been a delight to learn how well you have been going.

Now, to answer your questions about Cambridge University. Students there, incidentally, are called 'undergraduates' and then 'graduate' or 'research' students. So when/if you write, do not use the Australian term ('post-graduate') for the second group. In Cambridge there are graduate colleges (Clare Hall, Lucy Cavendish etc.) which admit only graduate students. The older colleges (Trinity, Pembroke etc.) have both undergraduate and graduate students.

There is no problem at any college about being married, Catholic and in graduate studies. But to get into a college, recommendations from your supervisor, maybe from myself etc. would help. I could help particularly in the case of Pembroke. Your degree with first-class honours is the best recommendation, of course. In general, Australians are welcome at Cambridge.

I don't see any particular problem about being admitted to do research by the Faculty of Divinity (St John's Street, Cambridge) on the basis of a degree in religious studies. More problematic is the question of finding a supervisor who is expert in Neoplatonism. My friends in the Divinity Faculty have specialized in other fields (e.g. Professor Nicholas Lash in modern theology and, to some extent, philosophy). When/if you apply to the Faculty of Divinity—write to the secretary—do mention my name and the fact that we are related.

Incidentally, apropos of applying to more than one college, I simply do not know whether as a graduate student you should do that. I can't see how it would do any harm, if you or anyone else applied to a couple of colleges. Trinity College, by the way, has some good housing for married students.

Cambridge is expensive, and there are few scholarships indeed available at the Australian end to get you there.

I feel frustrated at not being able to discuss this with you personally. My instinct (not very strong) is to let Richard Campbell [professor at an Australian university] supervise you and apply for a Commonwealth Post-Graduate Research Scholarship. The opportunity seems to be there. Say, in a few years time, your PhD done and with a job at an Australian university or tertiary college—hopefully, a university—you could take a sabbatical at Cambridge or Oxford (depending on where experts in your field are to be found).

[Nick was accepted by Emmanuel College, Cambridge, and, supervised by Canon Brian Hebblethwaite, successfully defended his doctoral thesis on Cambridge Neoplatonists. On returning to Australia, he spent many years teaching religious education for a very large Melbourne public school, Wesley College.]

24 June 1984, University of San Francisco.

Dear Maev, Welcome back to PNG! I hope the malaria bout is behind you and that you are feeling tolerably fit to face all the work again. I appreciate very much your reasons for not wanting to be nominated for the Al Schweitzer award, and I wrote to my French friend [Jean Leclercq] to tell him not to go ahead. Incidentally, there were no awards made in 1982–84; the committee had run out of funds. I hadn't heard from my French friend about it, until he wrote recently to say that they would be starting to make awards again in 1985, and he wanted to put your name up and re-open with you what he had begun in 1981, So that was the story.

The two days with Rick and Marion were very quiet and happy, with only one party! I was glad of a good sleep after my Atlantic crossing (my 22nd). I talked with the McDonalds [in New Jersey] after seeing [in New York] Joanna, baby [Douglas] and Bob (weekend of 4/5 August).

Last Friday I started my course on Jesus' resurrection; 35 have signed on, including a doctor (a neurologist) and a lady bartender. I have been trying to find the right answer for those (not students) who hear that I am teaching a course on the resurrection and ask: 'Do you believe in it? Did it happen?' I have tried answers like, 'It's the only object of my faith. I don't really believe in anything else'; or 'I believe in it obsessively. It's a major problem for me and my spiritual director.' But—seriously—it's a peculiar phenomenon the way people often react to hearing that I teach or write about the resurrection. They wouldn't say, 'Do they happen?', if they heard that I was teaching a course on the sacraments. Nor would they say, 'Do you believe in it?', if I told them that I was teaching a course on the Church. But enough of this.

My problem with the typewriter in Rome was that I was too lazy to change my corrector fluid; it was sitting there on my desk. I was rushing from one item to another at the end of the semester. But thanks for the concern. The machine [which I suspect Maev gave me] runs perfectly.

In a few minutes I am off to have supper with the local archbishop, John Quinn, an alumnus of the Gregorian and a great supporter [of Jesuits and their work]. I was touched by his kindness in phoning to ask me round before he goes off on holidays. Talking of kindness, I think of Giuseppe Lamaro, the youngest son of Maria Franca and Sergio, who drove me to the airport on 16 June. Since Christmas, he has been coming round on Monday for a little English conversation, and we have become great friends. I offered to do his wedding, introduced him to Sabina (Giorgio Barzilai's daughter) and told him it's up to him now. Giuseppe is coming through San Francisco en route to Los Angeles and the Olympic Games, at which his brother is representing Italy in the yachting.

I spoke to Justin [Peters, a nephew] on the phone, but no chance of seeing him as he moves to Miami and a new job at the beginning of July. He joked about always being on the road for his birthday [5 July].

I leave San Francisco on 4 August, spend ten days in the Holy Land, a week in Perugia, and then back to Rome at the beginning of September. Much love, Gerald.

2 October 1984, Gregorian University.

Dear Maev. Thanks for the Independence Day [4 July] letter. In New York I had a long Sunday with Joanna, Bob and the baby. They adore little Douglas, and I was very touched by Bob's articulate affection for the dear, little monster. All healthy babies look the same to me, and this one is definitely of that sort.

En route through Rome to Tel Aviv, I took in a Mass at the Fiumicino airport [on 15 August]. 'Just a thought (*appena un pensiero*)', the priest announced after reading the Gospel. Then he took us through the story of Mary from her conception to her assumption, reflected on the history of salvation, consoled us about our final destiny, and threw in for good measure a justification for the Pope going skiing with Pertini [the Italian president]—'the body shares in salvation'.

As we swept through new Jerusalem in a shared taxi, we passed a sumptuous building and one of the other passengers informed us loudly: 'A centre for children, paid for by an English millionaire, [Sir Isaac] Wolfson'. I thought that it was not the time or place to add that he is the first man since Jesus Christ to have a college named after him in both Oxford and Cambridge. The ten days in Israel were a wonderful spiritual experience. I want to return to the Holy Land as soon as possible. [The occasion of my visit was a meeting of deans of theology held at Tantur, an interreligious centre founded just outside Jerusalem by Pope Paul VI.]

Jim McDonald's mother has inoperable cancer. Orietta Doria (operated on around seven years ago for cancer of the breast) had a small tumour removed this summer. Enrico Massa—remember the bald lawyer-friend of Maria Franca [Lamaro]?—goes off for a heart operation tomorrow.

That's enough of that kind of news. 22–26 September, Rick's parents, Beau and Shirley Brown, stayed at the Hotel Columbus on the Via della Conciliazione. They liked my choice for them. We finished with a very late dinner out on the Via Cassia at the home of John and Mary Griffin. John runs Aer Lingus in Rome. You met Mary after the doctoral defence [of whom?] last December.

The theology of liberation is stirring them all up. Ross Benson, one of John Ellison's colleagues on the *Daily Express*, turned up on 20 September to interview me on the said theology. Benson's girl Friday also booked me for a show on American cable television.

A big hug and much love, Gerald. PS Our mutual friends, especially Giorgio [Barzilai] send you their warm greetings.

4 January 1985, Gregorian University.

My dear Maev, Tomorrow Dympna [our sister] and Dominic [her fourth and youngest child] arrive. So let me give you a Christmas report before they arrive. Betty Kilham Roberts has gone blind and returned to England. She was a big gap at the Dorias' carol party. God be with her as she struggles with that further affliction. Louisa [who?] and her family wanted to be warmly remembered to you. On Christmas Eve the weather was like Christmas Eve 1983. Maria Franca [Lamaro] and her family again came around to the English College for Midnight Mass. On Christmas Day I took the train—practically the only passenger—out to Marino to have dinner with Giorgio. I half expected to do the cooking, but around ten relatives were there, including his niece Anna who did the lion's share of the work. In the evening I was with the Jesuit scholastics at the [College of the] Gesù, where Saint Nicholas contended with the pagan spirit, the Befana. They sent up my theology of the empty tomb with the claim that I had been running a line on the empty manger

On Boxing Day Aideen [Archbold] had a large party for all the waifs and strays—in her new digs in the Doria palace. On the 27th I took a couple of visitors off to the English College for the pantomime during which one of the students managed to land a pie in the face of the new rector. I don't think Jack Kennedy thought that this was quite the done thing. But *Babes in the Wood* was a great success.

Before Christmas I had lunch at his home with Desmond O'Grady. Kieran was back from Brown University where he is finishing a doctorate in maths. Desmond, Aideen, Maria Franca et al. always ask after you with great affection. Desmond, incidentally, has befriended a fascinating English Benedictine who lives in a monastery in the Jewish quarter after having spent his childhood off the Piazza del Popolo. [During World War II, the same Benedictine served in the British army during the Burma campaign. He was in charge of some mules, which carried ammunition and other supplies through the jungle and up the front. 'The Japanese had better mules than we did', he complained to me.]

I decided 1984 had been the year of three ambassadors for me: the Irish one (Frank Coffey), Sir Mark Heath (representing Elizabeth II) and Sir Peter Lawler (from Australia)—all of them ambassadors to the Holy See. They seem to want to entertain me, and with them I occasionally meet Mr Wilson, the US ambassador to the Holy See. He was back and forth like a yo-yo between Rome and Washington in the weeks before the Presidential election, making sure, I guess, that nothing went wrong with the way in which many of the US bishops were delivering the votes for Reagan. Back in October, the

Lawlers had me to lunch in the Circolo dei Scacchi, a kind of Roman equivalent to the Melbourne Club. It's the only time I have been driven back to the Gregorian in a diplomatic car. But, being three in the afternoon, there was no one there to witness the return. Sir Peter has the habit of taping one's conversation. It's my chance of feeding some theological data into his reports for [Bob] Hawke [the Australian Prime Minister] and Co.

Peace and much love, Gerald.

5 January 1986. Gregorian University.

My dear Maev, Here in Rome it is a perfect sunny day. The Goodyear blimp is cruising ponderously over Rome and right now heading towards the Gregorian. Late this afternoon Enrico [Massa] and Maria Franca [Lamaro] will take me out to Marino Laziale to say goodbye to Giorgio [Barzilai] who is off to San Domingo. Maria Franca's eldest son (plus wife) is expecting a child in mid-January, and they have asked me to baptize the little girl (they know that already) during Mass in the parish church. I was touched by the invitation, as well as by the fact that they wanted the baptism done in the liturgically correct way. Gian Luca [Lamaro] is working in a bank now, and most happily married to a Belgian teacher.

On 30 December I took the train to Naples, and at once felt like Jack Lemmon (in *Maccheroni*) when I reached the main railway station. I wandered around the city to visit the various places that feature in the movie. To complete the picture, an Italian family I had never met before (father, daughter Anna, and her fiancé Salvatore) insisted on driving me to the station when I was leaving and all kissing me goodbye. People criticize the film for being full of Neapolitan clichés, but from my lightning visit it seems that Neapolitans are walking clichés. So what? They are a warm-hearted, affectionate lot.

When I wasn't playing Jack Lemmon, I was into the role of Aeneas. A priest friend (actually from the Abruzzi but practically Neapolitan from living there for over thirty years) took me to the Burning Fields (Campi Flegrei). At Cumae, where Aeneas (Book VI of Virgil's *Aeneid*) left his ships and sailors on the beach, I followed the tunnel he took down to the grotto of the sybil. But I came away without any oracle, as the said sybil has long since departed. Afterwards we drove across to Lago d'Averno where Aeneas descended to the underworld and where the Romans later had a splendid naval base.

To my immense surprise I have almost finished a fairly long book on the resurrection [*Jesus Risen* (Mahwah, NJ: Paulist Press, 1987)]. A couple of colleagues, one in sacramental theology [Phil Rosato, SJ] and another in contemporary philosophy, really tightened up the argument in the relevant sections.

Over Easter I think of slipping up to Tübingen. In the summer I will be in England for part of July and in Latin America for August. No USA this summer. Duty [as dean of theology at the Gregorian] prevailed, and I have to see Latin America for myself and also show the Gregorian/ Roman flag down there. It is a way, I hope, to let them see that at least some of us on the left bank of the Tiber don't believe that [Latin American] liberation theology is the work of the devil.

Much love, Gerald. PS Giorgio, Maria Franca, and the others send you their very best.

Maev in her doctoral robes (Columbia University) at a degree ceremony of the University of Papua New Guinea.

2

Letters from 16 July 1988 to 1 October 1992

16 July 1988, Pereira, Colombia.

My dear Maev, after a week in New York, which even included two working lunches about doctoral theses (with an Irish missionary at the University of Chicago and a Brooklyn priest who has just started at Columbia University), I flew down to Bogotá on 9 July.

An incredible welcome here in Colombia. I gave five lectures (on the state of theology and Christology) to the sixty bishops of Colombia, and repeated them for an audience of 240 priests. Owing to a strike of the major airline, I flew up to Armenia with Carlos Gonzalez (a Mexican colleague at the Gregorian who is also lecturing to the same audiences as myself) and the bishop of Armenia who looked after us that night. In the Bolívar cinema—everything is Bolívar in this country—*Crocodile Dundee II* was showing. Here in Pereira they are currently screening *Mad Max II.* Talk about the long arm of the Australian film industry! The next morning the bishop's driver took us through wonderful coffee country to Pereira. With great courtesy the bishop came along too—just to make sure we were properly delivered to Monsignor Arias, the vicar-general of the diocese who has been looking after Carlos and myself as if we were apostles from heaven.

In Pereira one audience of 160 priests, another of 40 lay persons and a third of 40 sisters [presumably they were 40 sisters ministering in the diocese] heard our lectures. Like the folk in Bogotá they put up with my poor Spanish pronunciation. In Medellín over 400 priests have signed up for our lectures. (I don't know the figures for the lay persons and sisters.) After Medellín, Carlos is going south to run a mini-course for the Argentinian bishops and then return to Colombia—for a further set of lectures in Cali, a city dominated by three bare crosses that rise on a mountain nearby. The whole experience here in Colombia has made me feel a bit like a latter-day (?) prophet being honoured outside his own country.

Like Armenia, Pereira is a great centre for coffee production, but also has some industry, above all a flourishing textile industry. It means that Pereira is full of boutiques and very well-dressed and pretty girls. On Thursday afternoon Monsignor Arias whipped us around town, not omitting the wealthy new suburb of San Martin where some drug barons live. On Friday afternoon he took me off to a sleepy, colonial town called Carthage. (Near here you have places called Turin, Palestine, Finland, Philadelphia etc.)

Coffee (including a new plant that can endure direct sun), bananas, sugarcane, pineapples and goodness knows what else grow around here in wild profusion. 'This must be the original paradise', I said to Monsignor Arias. 'There they are', he told me in the nearby city of Manizales ('a field of peanuts'). He was pointing out two tall bronzes of a man and a woman just on the edge of the main square ('Plaza de Bolívar'—you guessed it). The fertility and beauty of Colombia makes the endemic violence even sadder; guerillas killed fifteen soldiers last Tuesday; right-wing death squads are in action (they murdered a priest near Medellín earlier this year—his crime was educating and organizing the poor); the cocaine trade flourishes with all its mafia-style connections; the strong man of Panama, General Noriega, is a thoroughly destabilizing influence here in Colombia.

Yesterday the national games began in Armenia. Cyclists and athletes fill up the little hotel where Carlos and are staying. 'Land of hope and glory' blared out yesterday afternoon from television sets as the games were officially opened. Out the back of the hotel, just under my room, is a Hari Krishna community, 30 or 40 of them with their saffron robes and shaven heads. They were at the drums and chant from five o'clock this morning. Why have I never seen an old or middle-aged member of Hari Krishna? Is the movement restricted to the young? Much love, Gerald.

7 January 1989, Gregorian University.

My dear Maev, To start 1989 well, I decided to go for lunch on New Year's Day at the Oriental Institute (just opposite St Mary Major's). No three kings from the Orient there, but plenty of warm hospitality—in particular from a young Maltese professor [Edward Farrugia, SJ] who is writing a dictionary with me. To complete the approach to 1989, I took a break down in Naples (2–5 January) at Villa San Luigi in Posillipo. Naples may be dirty and violent, but it refreshes me always. Both the scenery and the Neapolitans themselves give me a sense of taking a box at the opera for several days.

Less than three weeks to go and first semester will be over. Then the run up to Easter is marked by frenetic preparation of programs and timetables. [I was thinking of my work as dean of theology preparing the academic year of 1989/90.]

All our friends here are well, both the oldies and the youngies. Laura [Zampetti] has five exams to do [at the University of Rome] before graduating. Leonardo [Ziliani] is busy with a dam up near Potenza. He and his young associates won a good contract for that job. At all events he is above ground now, having completed work on a sewerage system down in Taranto.

Much love, Gerald. PS Thanks for your card and news.

[Both Laura and Leonardo contributed chapters to a book on the Apostles' Creed that I wrote with young people from the Alban Hills, *Friends in Faith* (Mahwah, NJ: Paulist Press, 1989). Laura was interviewed for Chapter 1 and Leonardo for Chapter 3. Later I presided over his wedding to Donatella in the Church of Giovanni e Paolo in Venice and baptized his two children. Laura is currently heading the EU mission in Montenegro.]

10 April 1989, Gregorian University.

Dear Maev, Thanks very much for the letter of 19 March and all the news. Desmond O'Grady was glad to get your letter and comments.

All well here. I saw Enrico [Massa] the other evening. He is as cheerful as ever, despite his heart condition. Maria Franca [Lamaro] has fixed up a house for Giuseppe [the youngest of her four children] and reduced the size of her own home by selling a room to the next-door neighbour. Laura is almost at the end of her university studies. Desmond's daughter [Donatella] wants to get married in church. In that and many other matters, Desmond has the patience of Job.

A good holiday with you sounds just what I need. But, as I suggested to Dymps [our sister Dympna], could it be after Christmas? We work right up to Christmas, and I like a great sleep over Christmas (hibernation period?) to recover. Energy will be short at that season, given the heavy load I have to carry from early September. I will pop down to Sicily with Jim and Posey for a few days. But I hesitate to take on more. [This Sicilian visit with my brother and sister-in-law does not seem to have taken place.]

What about February? If it is not too late for you, the week of 11–17 February looks great for me. The exams will be over; second semester starts on 19 February. I have never seen Ravenna, Urbino, Ferrara, Modena, and Padova. Some good friends of mine live in Cremona. If we took the train to Bologna, we could hire a car there and finish the mini-tour back in Bologna.

Another possibility is latish July and the first part of August 1990. The first 2/3 weeks of July I am lecturing in the USA; around 15 August I am due in India for a meeting in Bangalore. In between, England and Scotland?

Back to Germany? How can I let my German turn rusty? The weather is obviously better in July/August.

Martin Molyneux (remember the vice-rector of the Beda [College]?) turned up the other day. Remind me to tell you the story about his brother in World War II. [His brother who spoke good German was moved to take charge of a low security, German officers, POW camp situated within an old castle. The Germans had discovered a good supply of whisky in the cellars.]

I leave Rome on 27 June for the USA, and arrive in Sydney on 28 July, Melbourne on 2 August, leaving for Rome on 24 August. In Melbourne I have asked for a room at Jesuit Theological College, 175 Royal Parade, Parkville, Vic. 3052. Any chance of seeing you then? Or maybe we can talk on the phone?

Much love, Gerald. PS In February maybe it is better to avoid the fog in Northern Italy and go down to Bari, Lecce etc.

18 May 1989, Gregorian University.

My dear Maev, Thank you for your April letter and a very happy birthday on 16 June. That day I will be starting a three-day meeting on science and religion out in the papal villa at Castel Gandolfo. The scientists attending are distinguished figures from the fast academic lane. So I plan to listen rather than talk, and will let my mind wander off to Papua New Guinea, hoping that friends are giving you a very congenial party. Know that you are loved and cherished by me, even if life keeps me far away on the Tiber Mission.

Apropos of the Castel Gandolfo meeting, I feel slightly cast in the role of a latter-day Cardinal Bellarmine (who once upon a time was professor and rector of the Gregorian), trying to repair the damage he and others did in the Galileo case. The Pope [John Paul II] would really like to lay to rest, for good and all, the notion that religion is against science. Contemporary disillusionment with some of the things scientists have been up to could help exorcise the old Galileo myth.

One sad departure and lots of happy arrivals here. On 30 April, Enrico Massa died and I said the Mass and buried him on 2 May. You may remember the bald lawyer with the heart problem? He battled on courageously and even went to his office the day before he died. R.I.P. [In the ambulance that took him to the hospital on 30 April, he cried out by name for Maria Franca and me.]

Yesterday Glynn and Barbara [my youngest brother and his second wife] arrived, full of the joys of spring. She is, as Moira and Dympna [our two sisters] described her, just the right person for Glynn.

A couple of weeks back two young women turned up from BBC 1, research assistants for Clive James. He is due in town at the beginning of June to film his third city of the year, the other choices for 1989 being Miami and Shanghai. Elaine and Karen wanted to locate a rich, decadent cardinal living in a luxury apartment and waiting to be elected pope. I told the girls that this species had died out centuries ago and that Clive was suffering from an excessive respect for past history. I gave them some suggestions and names of people Clive might like to interview. I hope to get into the act myself. The idea appeals to me—two Australians telling a British audience what they should think about Rome.

Last week fifteen Turkish, Muslim theologians spent several days here at the Gregorian—another first in interreligious dialogue. The rector of the University of Ankara came along and signed a covenant of friendly collaboration between his university and the Gregorian.

Yesterday I had lunch at the Russian College, a Jesuit-run establishment where we house Catholic and Orthodox students, all from Eastern Christianity. There are Romanian and Greek Orthodox students living there. The Russians are supposed to be coming back later this year.

Much love and a GREAT birthday party on 16 June,

Gerald.

1 October 1989, Gregorian University.

My dear Maev. Living in a foreign-language environment, I cannot decide whether it's more correct to say professor emeritus or emeritus professor [or professor emerita]. Either way, congratulations. I am glad the University of PNG recognized how much you have done on and off the campus.

Thanks for your letter from curfewed Lae [a town on the north coast of Papua New Guinea]. It's going to be so good seeing you and Dympna later this semester.

Did I ever mention that I got myself into preparing with a Maltese friend (extremely nice and bright, even if he looks like a terrorist) a concise theological dictionary. When we took off for the summer, we had reached 'heaven'. We have now resumed and completed the entries up to 'Jerusalem'. When I feel demoralized about the project, I recall the squads of lexicographers who have lived and died for the 350 dictionaries produced by Oxford University Press.

On 23 September I caught up with most of my young friends, out at Albano over supper in Elena Montani's house. Elena (now graduated from the University of Rome) and her sister Flavia (just graduated from high school) had wanted to plant a tree in the corner of their garden. They dug a small hole which caved in. They went six feet deeper and have excavated a Roman wall, some mosaics, broken pots, and a pile of bones—animal and human remains, including a patella. Elena and Flavia did not seem too keen about getting the bones dated by the carbon fourteen process. They might have the authorities descend on them, and their garden could be sealed off. Yet it would be good to know if the bones go back to the bold old days when Alba Longa had the Parthian legion quartered there. In any case the scene is intriguing, a small Roman dig at the bottom of a modern suburban garden.

The young people are impatient to see the book they did with me, *Friends in Faith*. It's due out with Paulist Press in a month's time. The Italian translation will be published soon after that. That industry functions efficiently in Italy—publishing. Twenty years ago they excelled themselves when the Italian version of Hans Küng's *Infallible?* appeared just before the German original hit the market.

Much love, Gerald.

22 May 1990, Gregorian University.

My dear Maev, my third visit to Sicily turned out

to be exhausting fun. On day one, we visitors for a symposium on John Henry Newman were bussed around to see Roman mosaics, fed to the teeth, and looked after splendidly by a bunch of uniformed young people. Day two was dedicated to the lectures, a Mass which featured a vigorous sermon by Cardinal Pappalardo of Palermo and more trips to the table. I have rarely been forced to eat so much in my life. The organizers liked my lecture on Newman's midlife journey being associated with or even triggered by his Sicilian experience. They invited me to redeliver it at Palermo on 30 May, when they will publish a collection of Newman's writing on Sicily (English on the one side and Italian translation on the other). I had to decline.

A very happy birthday on 16 June. I presume you will be in Melbourne then? That evening I will be at dinner with my painter friend, Giuseppe Crescimbeni, and will raise a glass in your honour. [In 1982 Crescimbeni did my portrait, which now hangs in the house library of the Jesuit Theological College in Parkville, Australia.]

I leave Rome on 23 June and via the USA and the UK reach Nuremberg on 30 July. I am not sure where Karl Holzbauer will have me stay. But the address is: c/o Dr K. Holzbauer, SJ, Caritasverband, Obstmarkt 28, 8500 Nürnberg 106, West Germany. Karl's telephone number is (0911) 235 40. It will be great to see you in Germany. [Maev came.]

Much love, Gerald.

21 June 1990, Gregorian University.

My dear Maev, Thanks for your letter of 18 May, and the flight details for your arrival in Nuremberg. The mayor, myself, and Karl Holzbauer will be in attendance at the airport—with captains and kings rolling out the red carpet.

I am not sure what Karl wants me to do—probably light duties like saying Mass each day in a [retirement] home. But we can get out during the day to Bamberg etc. There are lots to see around Nuremberg. It has great rail connections, part of the reason Hitler chose it for his new capital.

In mid-May I was down in Sicily for an international symposium held in a small town (15,000 inhabitants) called Leonforte. The town band, Cardinal Pappalardo of Palermo, and a good crowd of people turned out to listen to a number of us talk in Italian of varying quality about John Henry Newman and the 1833 sickness he suffered on his second visit to Sicily. He was down there, got very ill, started to find himself, and headed home (writing 'Lead Kindly Light' on the way) to set the Oxford Movement going. In 1833 Charles Darwin was off round the world, an outward journey in support of the theory of evolution. Anyway it was a welcome break down there in

Leonforte, even if it's the first time I have ever heard of, let alone participated in, an international symposium on someone's nearly fatal illness.

Just to repeat Karl Holzbauer's telephone number: Caritasverband (0911) 2354–0. That's just for emergency, as we will be at the airport.

Much love, Gerald.

6 November 1990, Gregorian University.

Dear Maev, I wrote to Nahau [Rooney] and hope this letter reaches you. October has come and gone. It was a good month. On the 13th a mega-Mass in St Mary Major's launched simultaneously (a) the Ignatian year in Rome (1990/91 being both 500 years since St Ignatius was born and 450 years since the Society of Jesus was officially approved), and (b) the academic year for the Gregorian Consortium (the Gregorian University plus the Biblical Institute and the Oriental Institute). The big crowd was welcomed by a Welsh monsignor, once a manufacturer of ladies' underwear and now the apostolic administrator of the basilica.

You remember the fabulous mosaics in that fifth-century building? Even perhaps the band of animals high above the altar? I saw those little beasts begin to scuttle off into corners when they heard some hunting horns. The 'Rallye du Parc aux Cerfs' came from Versailles, put on their scarlet uniforms, and blew their brass at four points during the ceremony. Later in the evening they were at it again—in Piazza Navona.

On the 20th I went out to Fiumicino to pick up a Lutheran bishop and his wife and bring them to the pensione run by the Bridgettines just off the Piazza Farnese. We hardly got in the door before Bishop Lohse met and hugged an old (Catholic) friend, Bishop Brandenburg (of Stockholm), who happened to be staying in the same pensione. Another first for me! Never before have I seen two German bishops hugging each other. The times they are a changing, not just ecumenically. A fine biblical scholar, Bishop Lohse is lecturing at the Gregorian for six weeks on Paul's Letter to the Romans.

On the 23rd I blessed the wedding of two young friends in St Agnes, Piazza Navona. The church and adjacent buildings may be taken over by Opus Dei money. But the Dorias, to whom the whole complex belongs, are fighting back. The case will be heard next month. Three of the four witnesses (at the wedding, not for the case) were women. More trustworthy than male witnesses? See the women in the Easter chapters of the four Gospels. With Mary and David hitched, I have gotten through my third wedding for the year, the other two being in Venice

(April) and Albano (June).

The month ended with a Halloween party just off the Spanish Steps. George, a journalist, had taped a horror film from the thirties to make the evening spookier. Boris Karloff and Bela Lugosi went at it hard until they were all dynamited, except for a young American couple who slipped back into normal life. One had to swallow a lot in that film—in particular, a splendid modern castle built in Hungarian woods on the site of a First World War battlefield. Were our parents and their generation easier to fool?

I am just off to see Pino [Castricella, a very disabled friend] in Velletri. Much love, Gerald.

[In the summer of 1990 I had joined Maev in visiting Prague. Later I wrote up for others an account of our visit.]

December 1990, Gregorian University.

My dear Maev, I thought you might like to see this.

My midsummer visit to Prague was a kaleidoscope of impressions that I want to share with you. By mid-August most of the bright young things of Europe and North America seemed to have converged on the city. It was standing room only on the Charles Bridge, which crosses the broad Vitava (Moldau) river to connect the Old Town and the 'Little Quarter', dominated by St Vitus' Cathedral and the royal (now the presidential) castle.

You could listen to hard rock in the Old Town Square or jazz on the Charles Bridge. Hawkers signalled a return to a market economy, and were selling a broad range of products—from traditional glassware to Red Army caps.

A Midsummer's Night Dream, billed as an 'erotic fantasy', was running from July into September. In late August the Rolling Stones came to town for a noisy success. Earlier in the same week the first casino opened

Under the hot sun, a general euphoria and tanned bodies made it hard to imagine the baton charges, police dogs, and water-cannon sweeps that occurred the previous November, before the nation finally 'straightened its back' and swept away the Communist Party.

On a corner of Narodni Street, where students were beaten during 'the velvet revolution', a theatrette offered hourly video presentations in English and German about those ten days and the events leading up to them. The films included some remarkable shots. A Communist Party official explained to a large crowd of factory workers that the demonstrators in Wenceslaus Square were just a pack of adolescents. 'We are not children', chanted the workers. 'Resign! Resign!' There were scenes of police, covered by helicopters, driving away visitors who had come to place flowers on the country grave of Jan Palach. As you remember, in 1959 that student had burned himself to death in protest in Wenceslaus Square.

Opposite the French embassy graffiti covered a large way of honoring John Lennon. In a dozen languages you were told to support truth, justice, love, and freedom. An elegantly written sentence caught my eye: 'peace in the world or the world in pieces.' 'Students were arrested for writing on this wall', an old friend told me. 'The government had those graffiti cleaned off each day. Yet people kept coming back to write more.'

But one did not really need the films or the graffiti to remember what the Czechs went through under the Nazis and the Communists. Smart streets have sunk into dust and decay. Many old churches urgently need restoration. Libraries and archives are in a miserable condition. The famous 'art nouveau' buildings have lost their brilliance. The whole country is desperate for foreign exchange.

You required no persuasion when told: 'The Communists left this country economically and morally bankrupt. Before the Second Word War we were among the first ten industrial nations in the world. Now we are forty-seventh.

President Havel's plays are being produced around the world. Across Prague, statues and monuments of

Kafka, Kepler, Beethoven, Goethe, Mozart, Dvořák, Emperor Charles IV (who founded the cathedral and the university), St Wenceslaus, St John Nepomucene, St Agnes of Bohemia, and others recall a spiritual and cultural heritage, but it has been almost totally submerged by totalitarian ideologies. Czechoslovakian culture has obviously taken a dreadful beating.

In the Old Town Square curious tourists giggled at the ugliest monument any of us are ever likely to see: a plastic car squatting on toad-like legs and celebrating socialist, technological 'success'.

I joined others who had escaped into the Tym Church for a moment's peace and prayer. A baroque organ, once played by Lord Edward Heath, announced the end of a marriage ceremony. A radiant bride and the warmth of family and friends reflected the optimistic message others had already conveyed to me.

Now back in the seminary of which they had been dispossessed for decades, the Catholic theological faculty of Prague was preparing for the coming academic year. Well over one hundred diocesan seminarians will live and study there again.

Despite economic fragility and transitional tensions, Czechoslovakian Christians and their leaders are planning the spiritual renewal of the nation. This is no easy task. A

Church of silence and suffering must be reshaped to meet the needs of the next generation.

The Czechoslovakian Church will not be alone in its efforts. Groups and individuals are already coming to offer their help. An old hand from a developing country [Maev herself], however, shared some misgivings: 'It reminds me just a little of a country experiencing a post-colonial rush of aid. Everyone has a solution. But both in Christian and national life, the local people must decide for themselves and work out their destiny.'

A university graduate, now retired, spends her senior years maintaining the Church of Our Saviour in its original baroque splendour. A middle-aged couple from San Francisco shared my joy at this ministry, which helps to keep that church a place of prayer for hundreds of students.

Dozens of bicycles caught my eye in the cloister of the Church of St James. They belonged to French boys and girls enjoying Franciscan hospitality there. A stooped brother, who for decades has guarded and cherished his monastery, radiated the joy of one who has fought the good fight and seen the tide turn. He took me through the sacristy into the church itself. In the sanctuary a novice master was leading four young men in the divine office. Faith is alive and growing in Czechoslovakia. Love, Gerald.

20 March 1991, Gregorian University.

My dear Maev. Below is a list of my movements that I prepared for various relatives and others. It may be useful for you. Thanks for your letter of earlier this month. At the moment I am trying to purge next year's programme of printers' errors. It is quite a job, as the languages the programme uses run from Latin to Polish! Valda [Creed, an Australian Carmelite friend of Maev] was through Rome last week and looked great. On 22 March I go out to Villa Cavalletti [in the Alban Hills] for a retreat, returning to the Gregorian on Easter Sunday.

Gerald O'Collins leaves for the University of San Francisco 17 May; returns to the Gregorian University 27 May. (I do not stop in New York etc.; British Airways takes me to San Francisco, with only one stop, London.) In San Francisco I am staying at the Jesuit Community, University of San Francisco, California 94117; tel (415) 666 0123. [I was visiting USF to receive an honorary doctorate.]

On 22 June he leaves Rome for New York to stay until 25 June at America House (tel (2120 581 4640). He then goes to New Jersey to give some lectures at an institute for priests offered by Seton Hall University.

28 June to 13 July c/o Theology department, University of Notre Dame, Notre Dame, South Bend, Indiana.

13/14 he is with Marion [Peters] and Rick [Brown, his niece and her husband] in St Louis, booked on TW 7489 (South Bend/St Louis), arriving in St Louis at 8.36 a.m.

On 14 July to the University of San Francisco; on 17 July out of Los Angeles to Sydney on QF 104, arriving Sydney on 19 July at 8.10 a.m.

Then I make my way (with Maev's help?) to Melbourne. Eventually I make my way back to Sydney, and take a QF flight to Perth on 24 August at 6.40 a.m. I am on a flight out of Perth to Rome on 30 August.

Around 19 September I go off to Madison, Wisconsin to speak at a symposium on St Augustine; from there I return to London around 26 September. From then until mid-January, I will be c/o Pembroke College, Cambridge CB2 1RF, UK. At the end of January I will be back in Rome.

11 June 1991, Gregorian University.

My dear Maev, There is no possibility of this reaching you in time for your birthday, but much love all the same for next Sunday. I hope there is someone there to celebrate it with you.

Your coming to Rome for my [60th] birthday [2 June] meant more to me than I can say. I am supposed to be a writer but words fail me. All I can say is that you made it an absolutely SPLENDID celebration.

Exams to the right and left these days. So far few incidents. With next Saturday's big finals [the comprehensive exams for the licentiate specialities], the worst will be over. On 22 June I leave for New York, [the University of] Notre Dame etc. Warm weather has really arrived here in Rome, and that, with the end of the academic year, puts smiles on many faces.

On Thursday next there is a garden party for the Queen's birthday at the home of the British ambassador to the Holy See [John Broadley]. So I can catch up once again with the Broadleys, Aideen [Archbold], the Dorias etc. before I leave.

Jared Wicks has just phoned; he takes over from me as dean of theology. So I must rush off; one must make the new dean happy, at least initially. Once again my loving thanks for your visit and a GREAT birthday. Much love, Gerald.

24 January 1992, Gregorian University.

Dear Maev, Just back from Cambridge and a couple of days in London (which included lunch in the House of Lords with Lord Longford).

Enclosed is a leaflet from the shop in Rome that Ron May [a friend of Maev teaching in Canberra with the interesting habit of collecting *liquori* created in Italian monasteries] was thinking of: ‘Ai Monasteri’, Piazza delle Cinque Lune 76, 00186 Roma; fax Italy + 6 + 689 6364. At the moment they do not have any posters, but they may get some if he writes to or faxes them. As Ron will see under ‘liquori’, there is a brand made out of eucalyptus by the Trappists of Tre Fontane. (Trappists are often called Cistercians.)

I would suggest that Ron writes to the shop, ‘Ai Monasteri’, for further data. The shop might forward his letter to their producers, since it is THE outlet in Rome for their products. I dare say the Italian consulate/ embassy in Canberra might help too.

I am beginning to plan my visit [to Australia] for July/ August ’93. Lots of love, Gerald.

22 February 1992, Gregorian University.

The Maltese are voting today in their national elections. There are no other elections; being so small, Malta has no town councils or other forms of local government. The prime minister is everything: lord mayor of Valetta, governor of Gozo, and the head of the highway patrol. Do you know the shortest book in the world? It is the Malta highway code. They told me that, with a smile. I think they are proud of their bad driving. Officially they drive on the left, but I was never quite sure. At all events, they don't drive too fast. They can't; otherwise they would head right off into the Mediterranean.

From all this you can see that Malta is on my mind, after giving three lectures for the University of Malta and one for the clergy of Gozo last week. They have, I presume, the smallest episcopal conference in the world: the archbishop of Malta and the bishop of Gozo. The apostolic delegate, nuncio, or whatever else he is called has a double brief. No prize for guessing the other country where he serves. San Marino!

During my visit I stayed in the seminary (at Rabat), occupying the apartment used by the Pope during his Malta experience of May 1990. Five nights in the papal bed did not do anything for me. The last night I dreamt of an eight-year-old girl, a child actress who wanted me to join her on the stage. When I shared this item over breakfast the following morning, the resident shrink [a priest psychologist who was also, I think, a spiritual director in the seminary] commented: 'The Pope was/is an actor, after all. Something was coming through there.' I thought it best not to share with the psychologist my stream of consciousness when occupying the papal throne, shaving in the papal mirror, and using the other pieces of equipment in the bathroom.

Did you ever hear of the Maltese hippopotamus? I saw several, or at least the skeletons of several in a museum. With deer, wolves, and elephants, they were active on the island around 300,000 BC. Apropos of the past, the Maltese remain outraged at a German who defended a doctoral thesis at [the University of] Bremen a few years ago and argued that St Paul never visited Malta. He [the German] transferred the story of the shipwreck [Acts 27:39–44) to Cephalonia. Some Maltese suggested that this pseudo-scholar was hand in hand with the Greek tourist industry and wanted to divert pious Germans from Malta to Cephalonia and the west coast of Greece. But do Germans come to Malta on pilgrimage (in the steps/ waves of St Paul) or to take the sun?

The second semester got under way last Monday. But, as you can see, Malta is still a happy, recent memory. Much love, Gerald.

[This letter refers to my brother Glynn, who came back from a cancer operation to win the 1992 Senior Championship at Metropolitan Golf Club, Melbourne.]

Easter Sunday 1992.

My dear Maev, Happy Easter and welcome back from Vanuatu [a country consisting of a group of islands in the South-West Pacific]. Maybe, however, you prefer Vanuatu to Canberra, especially as winter draws closer?

Glynn is as 'bad' or as good as Jack Nicklaus, who as a veteran managed, I think, to have some wins both in the open and the veteran category. On second thoughts, I am not so sure about the open category. At all events Glynn did very well against golfers over twenty years younger. That makes Glynn even greater than Nicklaus. [The year before, aged fifty-seven, in the final of Metropolitan's Men's Club Championship Glynn beat someone who was over thirty years younger.]

On 12 June I leave for the University of San Francisco (three weeks teaching), Dublin, Nuremberg etc., and back to Rome on 3 September. In Nuremberg (24 July–22 August), I am c/o Rev. Holzbauer, Caritas Pirckheimer Haus, Königstrasse 64, 8500 Nürnberg 2, Germany. I hope you like the references to Nuremberg in *Believing: Understanding the Creed* [Mahwah, NJ: Paulist Press, 1992; a book written with Mary Venturini].

A glorious spring day here. It makes the suffering and death of thousands over there in ex-Yugoslavia even more terrible. Much love, Gerald.

31 May 1992, Gregorian University.

My dear Maev, A very happy birthday on the 16th. I will raise a glass or two in your honour with Marion [Peters, our niece] and Rick [Brown, her husband]. As it happens, after leaving Rome on 12 June, I will spend 15/17 June with them in St Louis [where they both worked then for Washington University], before going off to teach (until 10 July) at the University of San Francisco, 650 Parker Avenue, San Francisco, California 94118, USA. From 24 July to 23 August, I will be at Caritas Pirckheimer Haus, Königstrasse 64, 8500 Nürnberg 2, Germany. More accurately, I will be based there, as I hope to spend much time of the time out in a village [Heldmansberg] with Karl [Holzbauer]. From 3 September I am back in Rome, helping to man the Gregorian mission.

Jim McDonald was through Rome recently, and we had a good chat over tea in the Piazza Navona. Maria [his daughter] is married and expecting a baby. Jim and his new wife (? Kathy) will be in Indonesia for four weeks around July.

If you get a letter from the University of Notre Dame,

Western Australia, apropos of the appointment of the next vice-chancellor, blame me. They wrote recently, asking for suggestions.

Today we had the canonization of Saint Claude de la Colombière in St Peter's. On the way back I stopped for lunch at the English College. In less than an hour the English publisher Stratford Caldecott is turning up—for a pizza with me. He is lovely chap.

Loads of visitors in town these weeks. Last Sunday I had lunch with the Archbishop of Canterbury, who kept calling me 'Gerry'. I found it hard to address him as 'George'. He reminded me that he had attended two of my lectures years ago in Rome.

Thanks for your April letter from Vanuatu. Much love, Gerald.

[Queen Elizabeth II referred to 1992 as an 'annus horribilis' (horrible year); it saw the collapse of their marriage for three of her children and a fire that severely damaged Windsor Castle.]

11 June 1992, Gregorian University.

My dear Maev, Thank you for your letter of 25 May which reached me on my birthday—a triumph of grace over the Italian postal system. Watch your ribs when jumping off boats! [Maev seems to have damaged herself jumping off a boat when travelling somewhere in Melanesia—presumably on some project for the Australian government or the Australian National University.]

As you can see, I am at my computerized workplace. I hope not to forget all I have learned (from two very helpful American neighbours on my fourth-floor corridor) about using the friendly beast. I fear having to start all over again when I return on 1 September. Tomorrow I take leave of Rome for the summer part of my pilgrim's progress. This evening there is the annual reception at the home of the British ambassador to the Holy See—for the Queen's birthday. (Poor Queen! She doesn't have too much comfort these days.) The party out on the lawn, with the walls of ancient Rome at the bottom of the garden, is a great chance of saying goodbye to friends and engage in public relations by shaking the hands of those who run the colleges and the Vatican. [The latter regularly included Monsignor Pietro Parolin, one of my former students who as Cardinal Parolin would serve as secretary of state for Pope Francis.]

I have finished a piece for the London *Tablet*, on the Pope's fundamental theology. If the term is unfamiliar, please check a recent concise dictionary. [I referred to the dictionary produced by Edward Farrugia and myself, *A Concise Dictionary of Theology* (Mahwah, NJ: Paulist Press. 1991).] The editor [John Wilkins] is a great friend.

I have to keep myself somewhat away from him, as I could finish up doing too many reviews etc. But maybe that would be a good idea. In general, however, I have tried to live by the advice Hans Küng gave me years ago: 'Write books, not articles.'

Karl [Holzbauer] and I will raise a glass to you in Heldmansberg [a village outside Nürnberg where we went in mid-August], Nürnberg, and other good watering places.

Much love, Gerald.

30 July 1992, Nuremberg.

My dear Maev, Karl and other friends in Nuremberg and Heldmansberg are asking after you. Karl has me doing the special sermon again on 15 August.

Our Irish friend Frank died earlier this year. RIP.

I will be back in Rome on 3 September, via England (where I am giving some lectures near Liverpool at the end of August. Thanks for your letter from Vanuatu. Much love, Gerald.

[Without trial, Frank spent years in a Northern Ireland gaol; eventually released, he was invited by Karl to come for a summer in Heldmansberg, the year when Maev had also joined Karl and myself there.]

21 August 1992, Tübingen.

My dear Maev, Thank you for your last letter which reached me in Nürnberg. Karl Holzbauer and other friends (including Josef and Ingrid Nolte) were delighted to have the latest news about you.

My month in Germany is over. Tomorrow I fly to Manchester and face several days of lecturing (in a summer course) before returning to Rome on 3 September. The fields and forests in the countryside beyond Nürnberg were as lovely as ever. The farmers had already harvested the wheat; potatoes were being dug; beet (half-embedded in the soil) and corn (standing high and majestic) were waiting to be brought into the barns.

In Nürnberg I helped out in two homes for old people. The summer garden-party at one of the homes ended with the arrival of a brass band. Most of the oldies had already gone back to their rooms, and they came out onto the balconies to be entertained by the young people with their trumpets, horns etc. below.

Do you remember the young couple (Peter and Marianne) in Heldmansberg who ran the church there? They have a little girl now (Charlotte), are expecting twins, and—much to the displeasure of the locals—are shifting to another post (in Ingolstadt). Karl sits under his huge apple tree—like a judge in the Old Testament—looks down the valley, goes for walks, and is as good company as ever. I pointed out to him the cradle-to-grave symbolism of the parish house (where P. and M. live) being attached to the church, with the cemetery abutting the far end of the church.

Every time I'm back in Germany I check the further importation of English into German. I noticed for the first time: 'eine clevere Alternative', 'Komfort' (slight change there) and 'das Airport Express'. 'Intercity' seems to have slipped, however; and the rail system runs more trains called 'Inter-regio'.

The TV carries much of the horror from Bosnia, alongside all the youthful beauty and bravado from Barcelona. German TV, thank God, is much more 'real' than Italian TV, which inflicts on us endless speeches from politicians

In a moment I'm off into Tübingen from Hirschau. Josef and Ingrid send you their love. They have Heike, the girlfriend of Johannes [their son], staying with them. Heike is just like Ingrid was, 25 years back, when she and Josef married in August 1967. Much love, Gerald.

[This letter refers to a nephew, Nicholas Coleman.]

1 October 1992.

My dear Maev, Just a quick note to assure you that I have booked you a single room at Santa Brigida (no curfew, key available, etc.) from December 28 for two weeks. In a fax to Posey [our sister-in-law] a couple of days ago, I said that I would be doing that. But now the deed is done; the room is ready. Santa Brigida is on the corner of the Piazza Farnese and the street leading to the English College, the via Monserrato. The cost for bed and breakfast is around 90,000 lire. A bit high, but it is a splendid place and the lire has come down a lot against the Australian dollar.[4]

Jim and Shirley Gobbo turn up this weekend, before returning to Australia. They have been in Italy for ten days or more. Talking of Italo-Australians, Ferruccio Romanin, SJ, has just arrived back, for a two-month stay in Rome. He will brighten us all up.

4 During her stay in Rome, Maev enjoyed one or two meals with the Prince and Princess Doria Pamphilj. On 4 February 1993, Princess Orietta wrote to Maev: 'Dear Maev, A thousand thanks for those beautiful flowers and your sweet note. You really should not have spoilt us. For us it was a great pleasure to see you and hear all your interesting news. Sorry to be so long in writing, but I have only just managed to get your address from Gerry. Life here goes on in the same happy, disorganized way. Our weather has been glorious; so Frank and I have done a lot of wandering around in the late morning sunshine. Hope we will see you back in Rome very soon. Do please remember that we have a guest room which we would love you to occupy if it ever can be of any use to you (so long as we are not away ourselves or someone else in it!). With our love and all good wishes, Frank and Orietta.'

Next weekend (October 9/10), Nick Coleman, plus wife and son Lachlan, will be overnighting in Rome en route back to Australia. On October 10, I am off to the USA to give three lectures, arriving back in Rome on October 22. At the opening of the academic year I wouldn't dream of doing a trip like this. But the key lecture is to the US bishops. So the dean of theology thought I must say yes. Much love, Gerald.

Maev in the honorary doctoral robes of the Australian Catholic University: April, 2019.

3

Letters from 29 May 1994 to 3 August 2017

[This letter refers to a number of young Italian friends, to their teacher, Mimi Sbisà, and her American husband, Lee Shore, and to my brother Jim and his wife Posey.]

29 May 1994, Gregorian University.

My dear Maev, A very happy birthday on 16 June, when glasses shall be raised to you on the banks of the Tiber and sundry other places. I had intended to do so after a wedding at Palazzola (the English College villa on Lake Albano), but Luca and Elena have now put their wedding off to a post-July date. You remember my *Friends in Faith* (Mahwah, NJ: Paulist Press, 1989)? He did the chapter on the resurrection and she did the chapter on the church.

They were up there yesterday, with Mimi, Lee, Leonardo,

and most of my other young friends—for Mass at 12.30 and then a leisurely picnic in the garden of Palazzola. They brought Pino along in his wheelchair from Velletri. He always asks after you. It's a grace having him here, as well as bringing the small children along. Yesterday there were three of them, playing with the tiny fountain, running up and down the garden, and pulling off their clothes to plunge into the pool.

Friends from different parts of the world have been turning up in Rome to enjoy the long days, the flowers, and the warmth of the sun (not yet violently hot). One came from the Leicester Polytechnic, now renamed De Montfort University. A couple arrived from London and invited me around to their apartment for supper. 'But where is it?', I asked. 'At the Spanish Steps', they told me on the phone from London. 'But exactly where?' 'Above Keats's house', they said. A marvellous spot to stay, if a bit noisy. You go into the house where Keats died, head upstairs beyond his apartment, and right at the top is a (fairly expensive) apartment for visitors.

On 1 July, I'm off to the USA (via a couple of days in London and Cambridge to see publishers and Jim/Posey), to Nuremberg on 24 July, and back to Rome on August 24. Much love, Gerald.

[This letter crossed a fax from Maev, who wrote from Canberra, Australia, on 1 June]:

> A Very Happy Birthday for tomorrow! This is just in case I don't reach you by telephone on the day itself. I am not sure if you have received a card from the wilds of the Highlands of Papua New Guinea. It was a very exciting, only mildly challenging, and thoroughly enjoyable five weeks.
>
> Last night I took the Premier of Manus Province to dinner, along with four other Manusians (I guess that is the right word). He has a Master's from Victoria University in Canada, and is delightful, long-time friend. It was great to catch up, and be able to repay some of his hospitality when I was a researcher in Manus in 1989.
>
> At the moment I have just finished writing an "expert" opinion on a remote area of the Southern coast of Papua New Guinea, where a port for an oil and gas pipeline is to be developed. At present it can be reached only by boat. If this New Zealand engineering firm wins the contract, I may be all set for another adventure. I shall keep you posted. Much love,
>
> Maev.

[This letter refers to my brother Glynn, journalist friend Desmond O'Grady, and Jesuit friend Karl Holzbauer.]

21 June 1994, Gregorian University.

My dear Maev, Today a note arrived from Glynn, saying among other things: 'Maev is on the mend, looking well, and should be out of hospital within the week.' Please God, you are o.k. You must have spent your birthday [16 June] in hospital. I hope all is well; no one said anything about your being laid up.

We are in the middle of exams here—hundreds of orals to listen to. There may be a shortage of vocations and students of theology elsewhere but not here. It's nice to be wanted. But six days of orals can tax one's academic stamina.

Desmond is not too good. No dramatic discoveries yet, but I can't help feeling that after so many tests they will find something malign in the poor guy. Perhaps I am affected by Nanni Moretti's latest film, *Caro Diario* [Dear Diary], which relates what doctors put him through for a year. He is a wonderful, 40-year-old Italian actor and director, who wins prizes at Cannes but is simply untranslatable into other languages. He is very Italian. After seeing his *The Mass is Ended*, a kind of Italian version of Bernanos's

Diary of a Country Curate, I spent an evening with him. 'Surely life is not that bad on the outskirts of Rome', I remarked. 'It's even worse', Moretti assured me.

I am about to write to Karl Holzbauer to fix up arrangements for a month in Nuremberg (24 July to 24 August). I leave Rome on 3 July and reach Nuremberg not by the most direct route—via Cambridge and New York. Much love, Gerald.

[This letter refers to the British writer J. R. R. Tolkien, the saintly American activist Dorothy Day, my niece Marion Peters and her husband, and the great Anglican scholar Henry Chadwick.]

9 September 1994, Marquette University.

My dear Maev, I hope this catches you before you take off for Papua New Guinea. Late summer is still operative here in Milwaukee, students look cheerful, and I feel liberated (with only a doctoral seminar to run and all the time in the world to read and write lofty theological thoughts).

Marquette has a Tolkien archive, the Dorothy Day archive, and a medieval chapel transported here stone by stone from the French countryside. Joan of Arc prayed in the chapel. It forms the lovely centrepiece of the campus, surrounded by trees, flowers (still happily blooming), and large urns.

I haven't spoken to Marion and Rick yet, but will remedy that over the weekend. I am just back from a guided tour of the University's library, and my head is reeling from all the CD-Roms which allow you to look up anything in the ancient and modern world: e.g., anything the Fathers of the Church ever wrote and any doctoral dissertation ever submitted in the USA.

A good friend of mine and publishing partner, Dan Kendall, SJ, arrives this weekend, en route back from the University of Notre Dame to his domicile at the University of San Francisco. In early October, Henry Chadwick visits from Oxford, to deliver the keynote address at a farewell to George Tavard, a distinguished French theologian who has been at Marquette for a number of years now.

Right next door to the Jesuit Residence at Marquette is the students' theatre, where movies are shown at least once a week. I caught *Schindler's List* last Saturday night. Ben Kingsley as a Jewish accountant practically ran away with the film, I thought.

I hope the doctors have got you absolutely A.1 by this time, and you can resume normal life. Much love, Gerald.

12 March 1995, Gregorian University.

My dear Maev, Happy days in Canberra, Papua New Guinea, Melbourne, or wherever else this letter finds you. One way or another, I hope you will be celebrating with Moira on the 23rd [her birthday]. I did write to her, but please give her again my very best wishes.

A lovely spring day here in Rome. Despite the economic and political crisis, a good crowd turned out for today's marathon. Balloons went up and good cheer was exuded on all sides. Viva Italia! Viva Roma!

I did some bookings the other day for the summer. I leave Rome on 29 June for the USA and Oz [Australia], arriving in Melbourne (Jesuit Theological College, Parkville) on 4 August. I leave for Perth and Rome on 26 August. Four tulips have been blooming away happily on my window ledge for a week or more. No rough winds or heavy rain have done them in—yet.

Recently I did eight recordings, 'Pause for Thought' for BBC Radio Two. The two producers, David Benedictus [a novelist and theatre director] and Jane Jeffes, [who later moved to Sydney and worked for the Australian Broadcasting Commission], did my technique the world of good. I now answer, or try to answer, the phone differently, being 'allegro' one day, 'allegro andante' another day, 'un po' melancolico' another day, 'commosso', etc. People will wonder what I am up to. But it's a way of practising my radio technique—at no cost. I'm warming myself up to record three or four pieces for Vatican Radio before Palm Sunday.

Several years ago an American seminarian (in first year) told me of dropping into an eating joint that was way out in the West of the USA. The radio happened to be playing and, even more remarkably, was tuned into the short-wave band for a Vatican Radio broadcast. He heard my voice! What he heard me say confirmed him in his resolve to study for the priesthood in Rome, and lo and behold he hears the same voice (in thick Italian) reaching him in first-year theology, the first day of the first semester. It all sounded to me like a story Uncle Gerald [a Columban missionary in China for many years] might have told. I'm not sure what happened to the seminarian in question. But what a start!

I may have to go into radio silence over the next few weeks. The workload is 'enorme', as the natives say around these parts. And I have to get some lectures ready for a Holy Week course I am to give in 'Ammerdown', a retreat centre in Somerset. I went there several times from 1974 to 1985, but have never been back since. It's a most beautiful place, just a few miles from Downside Abbey and the lovely village of Mells, where Monsignor Ronald Knox, Horners, and Asquiths galore are buried.

Peace and much love, Gerald.

[Knox (d. 1957) was a notable Catholic writer; in the sixteenth century, Thomas Horner, celebrated in 'Little Jack Horner', pulled out the pie by acquiring Mells Manor; Herbert Henry Asquith was British prime minister 1908–1916.]

[This letter refers to the Australian journalist and novelist Desmond O'Grady, to a friend Mimi Sbisà and her husband Lee, to a Victorian Supreme Court judge John Batt, and to my barrister nephew Jim Peters.]

8 April 1996, Gregorian University.

My dear Maev, The swifts are forming patterns over Rome, the Easter break has just opened, and it's about time that I write (before leaving to lead a retreat in England, April 10–20, down, or is it up?, in Somerset. The weeping Madonna of Civitavecchia fills the national newspapers ('They kidnapped the Madonna', bishop explodes) and gets good coverage as well on national TV. The Communist mayor of Civitavecchia has hired two ships to deal with the influx of pilgrims; magistrates have seized the statue pending further investigations (DNA tests on the tears of blood etc.), and the media continues to give the whole episode full and respectful hearing. The statue was due to be carried in a huge procession scheduled for Good Friday afternoon. Who knows whether the bishop will get the necessary court order and have the statue released in time for the procession?

My liturgical and para-liturgical functions seem tame by comparison. Last Sunday I baptized Giulia in the chapel of the Venerable English College. I had married her parents several years ago in the church of St Agnes (Piazza Navona). Why the chapel of the Venerable? Well, her mother had been baptized there thirty years ago, and her family has enjoyed all kinds of happy links with the College. So back we went. After I had filled in the books and put the vestments away, I stepped out into the Via Monserrato to ride around to their home (just off the Piazza Navona) on the back of the huge, red Honda that the father (Davide) drives (or do you say rides?). I felt the part, in my black suit and the vast helmet which Davide made me don. Sure enough, as we picked our way through the Sunday crowds strolling along the side streets, we ran into several Gregorian students, Americans who were rightly impressed by my daring. No chance of high speed, however, on such a short run down side streets. Now I know what I was feeling when all those Harley Davidsons ripped past along the roads of Milwaukee when I was at Marquette University in 1993 and 1994.

Desmond O'Grady dropped by yesterday and gave me

a copy of his latest, *Correggio Jones*. In a few minutes I'm off to an evening meal in the Castelli Romani, with Mimi, Lee, and a selection of the young folk. They will be pleased to learn that our book, *Friends in Faith* (Mahwah, NJ: Paulist Press, 1989) is to come out now in Portuguese, thanks to a publisher in Brazil. [The book expounded the Apostles' Creed, and drew on what thirteen young Italians had to say.]

I leave Rome on 29 June, and via Newark, San Francisco, and Sydney reach Melbourne on 4 August. I will be at Jesuit Theological College, Parkville, until 26 August. A bit short, but I will have two weeks of lectures in Perth [at the University of Western Australia and elsewhere].

John and Margaret Batt will be here in early May. Young Jim appears [in court] before him now and then, and John is perfectly aware that he is dealing with my nephew. John and I got to know each other very well at Melbourne University, and have stayed in touch ever since. Much love, Gerald.

[This letter refers to my brother Jim and his wife Posey, Orietta and Frank Doria, other friends, Mimi Sbisà, her husband Lee, and Jared Wicks, an American Jesuit colleague at the Gregorian.]

2 June 1995, Gregorian University.

My dear Maev, Thanks so much for your birthday phone call and letter. I'm glad that the Indian slides [made by my Father in 1919] have gone to the National Library in Canberra. Please let me know if you can find anything further about Father's time in India [with the British army] from the office in London. Years ago I went there and started research on his dispatches, but ran out of time.

The day began well, with Italian jets screaming overhead and spewing out coloured smoke to form the Italian flag across the sky of Rome. Even if the second of June is no longer a fully operative national holiday as the Day of the Republic (people ask: Which republic?), they still do something to mark the occasion and, unwittingly, celebrate my birthday.

J. and P. are full of beans, and I am dying to hear Jim's report this evening from his medical congress on male impotence being held at the Vatican. Tomorrow evening (Saturday) I say a Mass for them and the Dorias in the Palazzo Doria—which seems to please Orietta [Doria] a great deal. This evening we are going to Castel Gandolfo to dine, chez Buccis [a restaurant overlooking Lake Albano], with Mimi and Lee.

Next week I head off to make my yearly retreat, this time in a Jesuit retreat house in Ariccia, right on the old Via Appia.

A very, very happy birthday on the 16th. I will have exams all day, but in the peace of the evening will raise a glass to you, in the company of Jared Wicks and other chosen souls. Much love, Gerald.

[This letter refers to Terry Waite, held hostage in Lebanon for a several years, and the Prince and Princess Doria Pamphilj, and their children, Jonathan and Gesine.]

26 September 1995, Gregorian University.

My dear Maev, Enclosed are some items for you. The little folder on Blessed Dominic O'Collins [Irish Jesuit martyred in 1602] is meant for Jesuit breviaries. It was just published—a bit late [as he was beatified in Rome on 27 September 1992] but there you are. I thought someone in the family should have a copy. I hope this gets to you before you leave for Papua New Guinea.

Terry Waite has just done me a kindness by writing a foreword to the new edition of *The Second Journey*, about to be published by Gracewing, an English publisher. He didn't seem to mind my identifying his experience in Lebanon as a terrifying kind of second or midlife journey.

Next Saturday I have a wedding to celebrate in St Agnes (Piazza Navona), with the reception to follow in the Doria Palace. Diana Korach (who lives in the Piazza Navona) has been a friend of the Dorias since she was a child; Jonathan and Gesine will be witnesses. Frank and Orietta are astonishing. Neither of them are well, and yet they keep on doing things for others. Much love, Gerald.

[This letter refers to my cousin Monica Ellison and her husband John, Desmond O'Grady (an Australian journalist and novelist resident in Rome), and John Wilkins (still very much the editor of the London *Tablet*).]

3 December 1995, Gregorian University.

My dear Maev, A friend can carry this letter back to Australia to catch you before you leave for St Louis [for Christmas with our niece Marion Peters, her husband, and daughter]. My resolution for the New Year: stop criticizing the Brits.

How can I be critical of them? They have been so good to me, and especially recently. The service of welcome for the Ruddocks (the new couple in charge of the Anglican Centre) was a delight. I was so pleased to meet again

Mark Santer (the Anglican bishop of Birmingham and an old-Cambridge hand). After the prayers we went across the Via del Corso for wine and chewies chez the Dorias. In a bookstore last week I ran into Fr Michael Beattie, an English Jesuit out in Rome with a group of his parishioners. 'Why don't you come and stay with us in Farm Street [London] for a couple of months?', he urged me. Bishop James O'Brien (an auxiliary of the Archdiocese of Westminster) and Bishop Jack Brewer (Diocese of Lancaster) had lunch, also last week, at the Gregorian. I managed to steer Jack Brewer towards the topic of the villa used by the Scots College up in Marino Laziale and how he encouraged a seminarian from Glasgow to describe their red wine as 'Grotta Ferrata red'. When we meet, let me explain the story. It has to be wired for sound to get the full-blooded effect [a Scots accent struggling with the 'Rs' in Grotta Ferrata]. The British ambassador to the Holy See will have me back for dinner on 11 December—to meet various folk, including a friend of hers from Belgrade. A good change, as sometimes dinners in Rome feature the same crew. Invite the usual suspects?

Yesterday, at 11 a.m., I went out to the baptism of the Dorias' second grandchild, Elisa. An excellent, young Roman priest, Don Luca, who is a friend of Gesine's husband (Massimiliano), performed the ceremony; then we crossed the Via del Corso to the palace for a drink. I had two negronis! My last negroni was years ago, with Fr Philip Caraman [an English Jesuit, writer, and unofficial chaplain to various famous authors like Evelyn Waugh], and both Philip and I had two. You ARE allowed a little break towards Christmas. Frank's hands were so cold, when I held them in my warm paws. The life is going out of him. Then in the evening I went back to say Mass at 7 p.m. for Frank and Orietta. He read the second lesson pretty well, but had little to say over the evening meal. They are so blessed by their butler, Mario, and Orietta is wonderfully brave and caring.

I leave for London and Cornwall on 21 December and return to Rome on 31 December. Never miss the New Year on the banks of the Tiber? In London I will catch up with Monica and John, John Wilkins, and others. Desmond O'Grady is pretty cheerful; we talk once a week or so, and meet every now and then. Give them all in St Louis a big, Roman-Empire-size hug from me. Much love for Christmas and the New Year, Gerald. PS *America* magazine may carry an article by me in their Christmas number. [They did publish 'Filling Our Senses.']

[This letter refers to a Sydney friend, John Brophy, to my brother Glynn, to Desmond O'Grady, an Australian journalist, to a friend who lived at Castel Gandolfo, Mimi Sbisà, and her husband Lee, to her son Matteo, and daughter-in-law, Marina.]

4 March 1996, Gregorian University.

My dear Maev, I can hardly imagine the glee of John Brophy over the results of the national elections in Australia. [John Howard replaced Paul Keating as Prime Minister.] You must have phoned him, or maybe he phoned you. Please congratulate Glynn from me on winning the Seniors Championship once again [at Metropolitan Golf Club]. Poor Mike Fitchett, his old time rival! Thanks for the Australia Day fax.

Because I don't live in Australia, they threw me out of the Australian *Who's Who*. But I have been creeping back elsewhere, and hope that we are alongside each other in the *Who's Who in Australasia and the Pacific Nations* (3rd edn just published by the International Biographical Centre, Cambridge, UK).

Desmond is off shortly for a month in Australia, and showed me a copy of a lecture he will give on Australian feelings about living in Italy. I have been gathering memories for him, ones that convey something of my wonder and affection. Recently (on a Sunday) I went up by the little train to Castel Gandolfo. After lunch with Mimi and Lee, I headed back to Rome on the same little train, but had left my return ticket behind in the copy I gave them of the paper *Wanted in Rome*—something I discovered shortly after boarding and just before the ticket collector arrived. 'I had a return ticket', I explained in my best Italian. 'But I left it behind in a newspaper at Castel Gandolfo.' He shrugged his shoulders and went off down the train. In what other country could I have done that and enjoyed such a response? Yesterday I took a walk past the Colosseum and back to the Gregorian via the Circo Massimo. On the Via dei Fori Imperiali, a tourist party trotted by in an old horse-drawn carriage. The driver was talking to someone on a mobile phone. It just seemed weirdly incongruous.

Two cultural items appeal to me enormously: first, the way Italians telephone each other at 7.30 in the morning to plan the day. You may not make appointments ahead of time. They must be made or at least confirmed earlier the very same day. My fantasy is that half of Italy phones the other half at 7.30—to arrange their schedules day by day. As you know, Italian babies are much loved and cared for. I get fascinated by them when they are lying in a pusher, bound or rather encased in an excessive amount of clothing, their arms and legs stuck sideways, and their wonderful eyes swivelling around to pick out passers by. As I go past, our eyes often meet, and I fancy that all kind of great messages get communicated between the bambini and myself. Maybe they are practising very young for that extraordinary eye contact and swivelling vision of the grownups, especially the grownup males.

Don't miss a number of *Newsweek* that comes out around 30 March. Mimi, by the way, is a grandmother: Ludovica, born a month ago to Marina and Matteo. Much love, Gerald

[This letter refers to Sir James Gobbo, who was still governor of the State of Victoria, his wife Shirley, my brother Jim, and his wife Posey.]

31 May 1998, Gregorian University.

My dear Maev, Thanks for the phone call, the first for my birthday, and thanks for your gift which shall be turned into some liquid asset. GREAT news about the Australian Catholic University; I hope and pray that this comes off as expected. [She was to be appointed an adjunct professor of ACU and would, eventually, receive an honorary doctorate from ACU]. A very happy birthday on the 16th.

Visitors are pouring out of the skies these days. On Monday last, Jim and Shirley Gobbo arrived and we had lunch together. He will receive an honorary doctorate at the University of Bologna tomorrow, the penultimate day of class here at the Gregorian, which effectively blocked any chance of my joining him. On Wednesday a certain Patricia (plus several in her entourage) came from London; she is a visionary and since the 1980s has been receiving visions and locutions from Jesus and his Mother. The topic she presented centred on the millions of aborted children and the possibility of their being officially recognized as virgin martyrs. Shortly after she left, John Cornwell walked across from the Hotel Eden to take me off to lunch. He was back in Rome from Cambridge (UK) to do more work towards his biography of Pope Pius XII [the sensationalist and unscholarly *Hitler's Pope*]. John published a work on visions etc. several years ago, *Powers of Darkness, Powers of Light.* But I thought it best not to distract him by telling him about Patricia.

On Friday a senior American widow, Betty Voli, turned up with a bunch of fascinating, 18th-century letters from a young Roman nobleman, Virgilio Cenci, who took three years on a trip to Paris, Madrid, and London. She wants to publish an English translation of them.[5] After she went, Gavin D'Costa dropped by. An Indian, he teaches at the University of Bristol, and has been a visiting professor at the Gregorian the last six weeks. I provided the last instalment of his salary and an icon of three angels visiting Abraham and Sarah—not the familiar one by St Andrew Roublev but one that features Abraham and

5 On her behalf, I contacted the venerable London publishers, John Murray, who were famous for publishing that kind of work. John Murray VII replied and expressed his regret that times had changed; he could not publish the Cenci letters. In 2002, Hodder Headline took over John Murray.

Sarah much more prominently. Gavin, Beryl, and their two little children return to Bristol late this week. To round things off, a Polish priest, Marian, flew into Rome on Saturday and came at once to visit me. He is writing a doctoral thesis on my views about divine love and the resurrection. After an hour or more he departed happily (with a book and several offprints under his arm), and I left to say Mass for the Dorias. All systems are go for the visit of Jim and Posey who should be arriving at their hotel any moment now.

On 30 June, I leave Rome for a month in the USA, mainly at the University of Notre Dame to teach in their theology summer program. I return to Rome on 6 August, and leave again on 14 August for the Jesuit community at Marquette University, Milwaukee. Much love, Gerald.

[This letter mentions a Canberra priest, Julian Wellspring, whom I came to know during his studies in Rome, and Dan Kendall, SJ, from the University of San Francisco.]

11 October, 1998.

Marquette University, Milwaukee,

Dear Maev, It was good to hear about Julian's ordination, as well as the news about the conference on Pacific Representations. Next Thursday (15 October) I fly over to Boston and give a lecture at Boston College, returning to Marquette on 17 October. But the important date is Monday 19 October, when a young friend of mine, Fr Greg Mustaciuolo, is going to the Metropolitan Museum with Cardinal O'Connor for a meal. He hopes to persuade the folk at the Metropolitan to put on an exhibition of paintings and sculptures featuring Jesus right around Easter 2000, so as to coincide with the Incarnation Summit that Steve Davis and I have organized for Easter 2000 in New York, the last of these 'summits' I hope. [It wasn't. We did one more in 2003, the Redemption Summit.] I'm praying that the Cardinal and Greg, his private secretary, can pull this off for us. It would be nice to end the series of three New York Summits (1996, 1998, and 2000) with a bang. [In fact, at Easter 2000 the Metropolitan hosted a lecture by David Brown (then of Durham University) on Christ's humanity and divinity in twentieth-century art, followed by a reception for the seven hundred invited guests around the pool of the Egyptian Temple.]

This morning I attended the eight o'clock Mass in the Milwaukee Cathedral to enjoy hearing Archbishop Weakland preach. The Mass is broadcast on the local radio every Sunday, and I can understand why. He preaches in such a lively fashion, and the liturgy is done with dignity and joy. I had a word with him afterwards, and hope to see him with more leisure during these months at Marquette.

[His retirement in 2002 would be overshadowed by the news that, years before, he had conducted a sexual relationship with a male associate, and that $450,000 had been paid to settle litigation arising from the affair.]

The Episcopalian chaplaincy at the University of Chicago invited me to talk about Anglican-Catholic relations on 29 October. So I will do that, visit a gallery or two, and rush back on 30 October, as Dan Kendall comes for a weekend here. He has a so far undisclosed project. I strongly suspect that he has in mind to publish something in 2001 to mark my 70th birthday. Good on you, Dan. [What he had in mind became D. Kendall and S.T. Davis (eds), *The Convergence of Theology: A Festschrift Honoring Gerald O'Collins, S.J.* (Mahwah, NJ: Paulist Press, 2001).]

Apropos of Anglicans, the Archbishop of Canterbury [George Carey] wrote the other day to see whether I might manage to write his Lent Book for 2000. I hastened to agree. It has to be something on Jesus—for the millennium year. The publisher is HarperCollins; so at many removes I will be working for Rupert Murdoch.

Have a GREAT book launch on the 14th. I think Grandfather's letter stands a fair chance of being read to all and sundry at the party. Much love, Gerald. [I was referring to Brenda Niall and John Thompson (eds),

Australian Letters (Melbourne: Oxford University Press, 1998), and Grandfather's letter of 1897 proposing marriage to our Grandmother, Abigail Dynon. The book was launched in Canberra by David Marr, a friend of Thompson, who headed the Australian studies section of the National Library of Australia. Now retired from Papua New Guinea to Canberra, Maev attended the launch].

23 May 1999, Gregorian University.

My dear Maev, A marvellously sunny day here in Rome for Pentecost. Charismatics arrived en masse yesterday, and I hope that their prayers will bring a renewed outpouring of the Holy Spirit on everyone in the eternal city. We need it.

A very, very happy birthday on the 16th. It is still more than three weeks off, but I wanted to make sure this letter reached you before you leave for Papua New Guinea. I hope your ex-students and other friends up there put on a fantastic celebration or two for you. I will be starting examinations that very day: 180 or so orals, 65 or so written exams. But it will be the first day, and I will certainly be fresh and strong enough to raise a glass to you at lunch.

Do you remember Bill Burrows, a Society of Divine Word priest who taught at Bomana [the seminary outside Port Moresby in Papua New Guinea], left, and became some years ago the head of Orbis Books (just outside New York)? You (or someone else?) took me up to Bomana in the 70s. Burrows turns up tomorrow and will host Jacques Dupuis and myself at a meal. It is the least he can do for old Dupuis, whose latest book has come under fire from the Holy Office, and is now into a paperback edition with Orbis. [Cardinal] Ratzinger and Co. really boosted the sales of the book, which came out simultaneously in English, French, and Italian at the end of 1997. I have enjoyed acting as Dupuis's consultor. It's a somewhat uneven encounter, which Ratzinger stretches language to call a 'dialogue'. They [the Congregation for the Doctrine of the Faith] hold some power, but show a gross lack of theological competence in the charges they have brought against Dupuis. He wrote (and then sent them in January) a marvellous 180-page reply to their charges, a reply that could be adapted and become a useful book, as a fine summary of his original 433-page book. I must suggest that tomorrow to Burrows.

Last Tuesday I had an evening meal with Jonathan and Gesine Doria, the first time the three of us have ever sat down together by ourselves. In a way that was most moving they talked about their parents, Frank, who died last October, and Orietta, who battles along with cancer. I wrote part of Frank's obituary for the *Tablet* and, with help from Jonathan and Gesine, am putting together one for Orietta. As I leave Rome on 28 June, spend a couple of weeks teaching in the USA, and then six weeks or so in Melbourne, I want to have the text ready and approved by J. and G. before I leave the banks of the Tiber and the sheltering walls of ancient Rome. Once again a very GREAT birthday. Much love, Gerald.

[This letter refers to a dear friend from Melbourne, John Batt; he and his wife flew in from Australia to celebrate my 75th birthday and departure from Rome.]

11 June 2006, Gregorian University.

Dear Maev, Here is our schedule. Monday June 12, we are both invited to dinner by Tracy Wilkinson and her husband. I think his name is O'Connor. She is the *Los Angeles Times* correspondent in Rome, and is writing a book on exorcism. We are due at 8 p.m., and their apartment is within walking distance of your pensione. What if I arrive at your pensione around 7.15; we can have a chat and then walk around to their apartment.

Tuesday 13 June: party with Gesine Doria and her husband Massimiliano Floridi, plus 35 others, including

Dan Kendall [Jesuit friend from San Francisco]. I can come to your pensione around 7.30, and we will wander off to the Doria Palace.

Wednesday 14 June: reception at the British Embassy to the Italian Republic, in honour of the Queen's Birthday. I can come around at 6.30 and we head there together.

Thursday 15 June: Irish College reception hosted by Mary Wilsey [Venturini] and Maggie Mason [founders and editors of *Wanted in Rome*]. It starts at six; so I had better be there by 5.45 or so.

Friday 16 June: 8 p.m. dinner at the Abruzzi restaurant, very close to the Gregorian. Our waiter is nicknamed 'il principe delle tenebre (the prince of darkness)'.

Sunday June 18: twelve o'clock at the Gregorian, for lunch with John and Margaret Batt. [The rest of the letter is lost.]

3 August 2017, Jesuit Theological College, Parkville

Dearest Maev,

Last Tuesday a visiting Italian professor (now with a chair at Villanova; University, near Philadelphia) came for the evening meal; he has the splendid name of Massimo Faggioli, which you might translate as Biggest Beans.

He is an exuberant person, and has been out lecturing in Sydney, Melbourne, and Adelaide. His favourite topics are Pope Francis and the Second Vatican Council, and he has me writing a chapter for a large book he is co-editing, *The Oxford Handbook of Vatican II* [published late 2022].

It's certainly the season for visitors from the Northern Hemisphere, with Steve, Marianne, and Samantha through for a long weekend en route to skiing in New Zealand. Last Friday Steve spoke during the students' dinner at Newman College (marking the start of the second semester) on being an engineer in Cambodia. His speech also included information about with the setting up of a national rugby team in Cambodia.

For years I have collected ads featuring the theme of 'life'. The latest one turned up recently at the Melbourne airport. It featured a medical doctor saying: 'I'm not just a GP. I'm your life specialist.' I continue to read the poems of Clive James, who has been dying on stage now for several years. He's a man who has nothing but poetry left.

I have just corrected the proofs for two books, with one more set of proofs to come imminently. They will lift my score of books published to 71, which is clearly excessive, if not obsessive.

Much love, Gerald.

Epilogue

Most of the letters this volume reproduces were written in Rome; a few came from where I found myself (often during breaks in the academic life of the Gregorian University) in Australia, Germany, India, Latin America, or the USA.

The letters show me relaxed and at home with Maev, constantly implying that we were both missioned people—Maev on her Papua New Guinea mission and myself on what I called ‘my Tiber mission’. That sense of a common mission, and not merely sibling love, made it easier to write about people and events that, I instinctively knew, would interest Maev.

The letter I wrote to her on the anniversary of her death makes the happiest and best epilogue to this book.

3 July 2022

Dearest Maev,

A year after your passing to the Lord on 3 July 2021, we miss you as much as ever, especially on the big occasions. On the morning of 18 May, I took myself off to a convention centre on the south bank of the Yarra for Annie Coleman's graduation at Australian Catholic University and then a festive lunch right near the chambers of our very busy KC nephew Jim Peters. Yes, he turned up and chose a quick sandwich. The trattoria where we ate nestles in an old factory and is named 'Scugnizzo (street urchin)'. You would have added even more fun to that family meal. Annie, by the way, started nursing months ago just down Royal Parade from me, at the Royal Melbourne Hospital.

For the ceremony itself, she wanted me to don the robes of my honorary doctorate at the ACU, join the official procession, and sit on the platform. I always take delight that you and I were both appointed adjunct professors of ACU and both received honorary doctorates from ACU. Will recognizing in this way a brother and sister remain an unchallenged double at ACU for years or even for ever?

You will have joined me in welcoming Australia first prime minister of Italian background, Anthony Albanese. Benvenuto e tanti auguri!

You would have also delighted in the latest publication by Nevie Peters [Jim's second daughter]: ten letters she wrote to me which are now reproduced in a volume (*Letters from the Pandemic*) that Connor Court has just put out. On 13 September the book will be officially launched at Newman College by Archbishop Philip Freier, the Anglican Archbishop of Melbourne. [COVID 19 brought, however, the cancellation of this official launch.]

Some weeks back I discovered in my study a batch of letters that I wrote to you (1978–2017) and have put them together into this book. Some of those letters mention friends who since your own death have also left us: Jim Gobbo, Desmond O'Grady, Monica Ellison, and John Wilkins. I attended Jim's state funeral held in St Patrick's Cathedral, and could also follow through streaming the Masses for Monica in the parish church of Wimbledon and for John in his London parish (Pimlico). At Monica's funeral I contributed a prayer which was read over her coffin.

As the last one standing of us six siblings, I've had to negotiate the loss of some of the best friends who shaped my life. In the case of Jim's passing, the governor of Victoria held a cheerful reception in the grounds of Government House. The ancient Italian who runs University Café in Lygon Street (Carlton), Gian Carlo, attended the reception and evoked all those lunches at which he fed me and Jim over many years. On 8 July, I will celebrate Les Coleman's independence day by lunching da Gian Carlo. Les is retiring from Melbourne

University's Department of Finance, leaving behind all those exams and other commitments.

Apropos of the past, on 17 June I returned to our parental home, 'Rock Lodge', for a lunch with the present owners, George and Kathy Beraldo. Stewart and Justin Peters brought me down when they heard of the visit. As boys they spent so many happy weekends there with their grandparents in what is now called Frankston South. The past brought back the good news—not least your driving loads of nephews and nieces on swimming and fishing expeditions.

George and Kathy let us glimpse something of the hospitality that Father and Mother taught us to practise. G. and K. have kept the old house in splendid condition, and revelled in the joy which the three of us showed in returning to our roots and early years. The spirit of 'Rock Lodge' lives on.

I look forward to catching up shortly with Lotte, Hugo, and Mietta. They will be visiting Melbourne with Tori from Singapore [a niece]. Lotte has just finished, or is just finishing, her school exams. I don't know yet what university she aspires to.

Living now in your final home with God, you must know all this news already. But just in case not everything has come through, I decided to include a report with this letter. Please pass on my love to Mother, Father, and all the relatives and friends who are enjoying with you a supremely happy life.

Very much love and see you soon, Gerald.

PS The other day I came across a disturbing view from Hannah Arendt: 'it is in the nature of the political realm to be at war with truth in all its forms' (*Truth and Politics*, 1967). You and I have so much to contemplate together and understand about God, truth, and the human condition.

PPS Do you remember our last meeting, when I flew up for a day from Melbourne to Canberra just before Christmas 2019. Terrible bushfires had made the air almost unbreathable. COVID 19 was about to strike and lock us down for well over a year. We both sensed that this could well be the last time we met on earth. At the airport you said nothing but gave me a mega-hug. With apologies to St Thomas More, I never loved you more than when you hugged me last.

Maev with Gerald at her 90th birthday party in Canberra: 16 June 2019.

Appendix I
Biography of Maev O'Collins

by her nephew Les Coleman

Ellen Maev (Maev) O'Collins, educator and social worker, was a second generation Irish-Australian, born on 16 June 1929 in Brighton, Victoria at the home of her parents Joan and Patrick Francis ('Frank') O'Collins.

Maev's mother was the oldest daughter of Patrick McMahon Glynn, an active member of the federal conventions that produced the Australian constitution, and a member of the first Australian Parliament who would hold several ministerial appointments including Attorney General. He was the last of the founding fathers to sit in the House of Representatives.

Joan was always an inveterate traveller, journeying alone on the Trans Siberian Railway and to locales as far flung as Iceland and Zambia. Maev's father served with the AIF on the French front and with the Indian Army in the Third Afghan War. He practised as a lawyer in Melbourne, developed several of Melbourne's first picture theatres, and became Deputy

Chairman of Colonial Mutual Life Assurance Society.[6] Maev inherited a spirit of adventure from her parents, and throughout her life invariably chose to follow `the road less travelled'.

Soon after Maev's birth, her family moved to a hilltop property five kilometres inland from Frankston, in an area then called Mt Eliza and now Frankston South. The isolation forged strong ties with her two older sisters and three younger brothers, and saw Maev start school at home under a governess. She then attended several convents, completing her Matriculation at Sacré Coeur, Glen Iris in 1945. She later completed a Bachelor of Arts at the University of Melbourne and a Graduate Diploma in Social Studies at Sydney University.

In 1952 Maev joined Catholic Social Services in East Melbourne and began a 16 year association with an organisation that grew into the Catholic Family Welfare Bureau. She was appointed Principal Officer Adoptions and helped hundreds of children and couples become happy families. With other social workers, Maev developed a model code of practice for adoptions that eventually became the basis for legislation that better protected the rights of adopting mothers and their children.

During this time Maev gave guest lectures at the University of Melbourne and seminars to professional associations that sparked her interest in further studies. In 1967 she was awarded a scholarship by the American Association of University Women

6 Frank O'Collins was responsible for the building of the Astor in St Kilda, still preserved as an example of 'art deco' in greater Melbourne.

to study in the United States. She completed a Master of Social Work at Columbia University in New York, and then a Doctor of Social Work in 1971. Her dissertation was entitled 'Policy Formulation in Australian Education: The establishment of the advisory committee on the teaching of Asian languages and culture in Australia'.

Maev stayed at International House for most of her time at Columbia University and forged lasting friendships with people from many countries. One of the most significant meetings was with Michael Somare (later Sir Michael and Prime Minister of Papua New Guinea), who was visiting New York as a young member of a delegation to the United Nations. Maev took him to dinner, where Somare invited her: 'Come and work for us at the new university in Port Moresby. Then if you get sick of us or we get sick of you, it's not far to go home.'

Maev laughed politely, but then Papua New Guinea began `calling', and in 1972 she started work at the University of Papua New Guinea as the first member of its Department of Social Work (later, the Department of Anthropology and Sociology). She soon ran into Somare, now Chief Minister, who greeted her warmly: 'I am glad to see you took my advice!'

Maev quickly steered the structure of the social work course towards fostering development, embracing concepts of social justice, and eradicating neo-colonialism. The last included many colonial-era structures that survived political Independence, and included codes and university administrative arrangements that were suitable for inner Sydney but blind to cultural obligations of local students. Her research interests centered on social and community development, which ensured their inclusion in planning PNG policy and projects. She was appointed professor in 1979.

In 1987 Maev was awarded an MBE by the PNG government 'for services to the community and education'. She took great pride that amongst the many letters of congratulation was one from Sir Julius Chan, another PNG Prime Minister, who said he was 'fully aware of the work, thought and affection you have given Papua New Guinea and her people over the years'. Two years later Maev left the university after reaching mandatory retirement age, and was awarded the title Emeritus Professor.

Maev continued as an active consultant for PNG to the United Nations and other international bodies. One of the roles she most enjoyed was with police training. This had begun in 1974 through teaching in the university's Diploma of Police Studies and continued for almost a decade after 1988 as advisor on social and cultural issues to an AusAID sponsored, police development project. This took her around Melanesia and—apart from generating a wealth of stories, sometimes chilling—gave her many opportunities to promote development.

After leaving the University of PNG, Maev settled in Canberra, taking up an appointment as Honorary Visiting Fellow at the Australian National University in 1990. She retained strong links to Papua New Guinea and its neighbours, and Maev's expertise was valued in Canberra. She supervised many postgraduate students from around the Pacific and Asia, and was involved in numerous studies, development projects, and consultancies.

During the 1990s she testified several times before the Australian Parliament's Joint Standing Committee on Foreign Affairs, Defence, and Trade in relation to topics including the Bougainville peace process and Australia's relations with PNG. She also shared her experience generously, ranging from talks to organizations providing aid to PNG such as the Rotary Club to seminars advising Australian Federal Police who were headed to the Solomon Islands.

In 1996 Maev took great delight in joining her sister Dympna to follow Alfred Wainwright's *Coast-to-Coast Walk* across England from the Lake District to Robin Hood's Bay. Later they planned to walk the entire course of the river Thames, but were forced by Dympna's illness to abandon the project.

Maev's academic career had been devoted to social issues in the south-west Pacific, and she serendipitously found a family connection in her maternal grandfather's role in the evolution of Norfolk Island's government during his time as Australian Minister for External Affairs. This research led to publication in 2002 of *An Uneasy Relationship: Norfolk Island and the Commonwealth of Australia*. In the meantime, Maev had also joined the staff of Australian Catholic University, and—when her brother Gerald received a similar appointment in 2009—they became the only brother-sister adjunct professors in the history of the university.

To the end of her life, Maev used her unique blend of experience in social work, community development, and stimulating cultural encounters to examine and share in national and international social justice and human rights issues. She continued to support a series of initiatives to promote understanding and acceptance of different cultures.

Appendix II:
Writing Letters by Gerald O'Collins

The correspondence (68–44 BC) between the Roman orator, philosopher, and politician Marcus Tullius Cicero, and his friend Titus Pomponius Atticus provides a rich, even unique source of information about the period when the Roman Republic fell and the Roman Empire emerged. Cicero revealed himself and his views of contemporary events and political figures in a remarkably frank way that meant that the collection of more than 900 letters was not published until years after his death. I am no Cicero, and not in danger if I publish letters during my lifetime. But sometimes I wonder whether my commitment to writing and collecting letters has been, at least in part. unconsciously prompted by unease over a period of world history when democracies are falling apart and oligarchies or worse are emerging.

I started gathering and publishing letters years ago. It was not enough to write a life of my maternal grandfather, Patrick McMahon Glynn (1855–1931) and put out his biography in 1965 with Melbourne University Press. Within a decade, letters followed. Polding Press published *Patrick McMahon Glynn: Letters to his Family (1874–1927)* in 1974. His first letter describes his pilgrimage as a nineteen-year-old to the shrine of the Virgin Mary at Lourdes in southern France. Mostly the letters came from the years after he sailed to Australia in 1880. Settling in South Australia, he began practicing as a lawyer and entered state politics. He took part as an chosen delegate in drafting the Australian federal constitution, and was elected to the national House of Representatives in 1901. After serving as a minister in three Commonwealth government, he was defeated in the 1919 elections, being the last of the 'founding fathers' to sit in the Commonwealth Parliament.

My family was delighted that Brenda Niall and her co-editor of the 1998 *Oxford Book of Australian Letters* included the letter Paddy Glynn wrote proposing marriage during the Federal Convention that produced the Australian constitution, He enlivened proceedings at the second session by suddenly risking 'the inevitable question' with Abigail Dynon of Melbourne, rushing down from Sydney to do so, and then returning at once with his bride to the proceedings of the Convention.

A couple of decades later, *The War Letters of Sir John Monash* appeared in 2015. My father had served under him on the French front during the First World War. The success of this collection of letters encouraged me to be even more interested in letters both as a form of literature and a source for historical writing.

Letters to Camondo by Edmund de Waal, the bestselling author of *The Hare with Amber Eyes*, came out in 2021 and has increased my admiration of letters as an art form. Finally, 2022 witnessed the publication of the correspondence between the American writer and political activist Robert Ellsberg and the English hermit and art critic Sister Wendy Beckett. Both of these recent publications deserve their success and have served to confirm my passion for publishing letters.

In 2016, St Paul's Publishing (London) put out my *Letters to Nevie.* This grandniece, Genevieve Peters, whom I christened as a baby back in 2,000, has acted as my muse in letter writing. She was the recipient of one letter in *Letters from Rome and Beyond* (Connor Court Publishing, 2021). *Letters from the Pandemic* (Connor Court Publishing, 2022) contained other letters to her and ten letters by her.

An American poet, Randall Jarrell (1914–1965), said: 'Writing poetry well is only occasionally difficult; usually it's impossible.' Could what Randall Jarrell said of poetry be applied to writing letters? Writing letters well is only occasionally difficult; usually it's impossible.

A friend of mine used to talk of situations being 'fraught'—fraught with risk, danger, or at least the possibility of undesirable outcomes. Fraught situations are those that, even (or especially) unintentionally, can cause anxiety and distress. Choosing and editing letters for publication create a situation fraught with risk.

Those who read the latest three volumes of letters I have published could well ask: Where are the letters *from* his sister Maev? She was a great friend and companion in my life. She did send me many astonishing letters during her years in New York and later in Port Moresby. Why did I fail to keep those letters? I have no ready explanation.

The failure looks even worse when I recall our beloved elder sister Moira (Peters). She kept *everything*, even the boarding passes for international flights she took over the years with her dear husband, Jim Peters.

Yes, writing letters well is only occasionally difficult; usually it's impossible. But it's always worth trying to write letters well. Whatever else you achieve, you show that you respect, and even love, the person you are writing to. In any case, you will be doing your best to keep up the standard of the English language.

Index

www.ingramcontent.com/pod-product-compliance
Ingram Content Group UK Ltd.
Pitfield, Milton Keynes, MK11 3LW, UK
UKHW020418250726
13967UKWH00007B/2711

9 781922 815446